THE JUNGLE TIDE

THE JUNGLE TIDE

JOHN STILL

GYAN

Published by

GYAN

Gyan Publishing House
5, Ansari Road
Daryaganj, New Delhi-110002
Phone: 011-47034999, 9811692060
E-mail: books@gyanbooks.com

Distribution Network
gyanbooks.com
India, USA, Canada, UK, Australia, France

ISBN : 978-81-212-4564-7 (HB)
First Published, London, 1930

2nd Impression 2020

Printed at: Gyan Press, Delhi.

The Jungle Tide
Author: John Still

THE
JUNGLE TIDE

by

JOHN STILL

WITH FRONTISPIECE

WILLIAM BLACKWOOD & SONS LTD.
EDINBURGH AND LONDON

[*Photograph by* E. MABERLY BRYDE.

ADAM'S PEAK.

To

H. R. FREEMAN

Knight-errant, and champion
of the Jungle Peoples' rights

CONTENTS

THE MOON

The moon looked through the boughs to me,
All new, and curved as though she smiled :
I moved my head aside to see,
And turned my treasures, like a child,
So who can say she brought no luck to me ?

I. A TIMBER RESERVE

I WELL remember the first time I entered a jungle. The planters of coffee and then of tea had cleared the valleys of their primeval forests, and stark uniformity, duller than a market garden, had taken their place except where, in ravines or swamps too steep or too wet for tea, wild scrub still harboured a few mongooses, a few wild cats, rare porcupines, and rarer jackals. But here and there on the hill-tops prudent planters had left small patches of the ancient woods untouched as timber reserves, whose most interesting function was to offer a last refuge to a few wild animals whose habits required larger sanctuaries than those of the ravines. Wild pigs were to be found in them, and families of the deep-voiced wanderoo monkeys; and of the deer tribe the little muntjac was common, and even the great sambhur, as large as a pony, not unknown. Eagles built their nests there in the tops of age-old trees, whose towering forms stood like giants looking out over scores of miles of hills and valleys, once the home of ten thousand of their kind, but now given over to tea, a humble white-flowering camelia, precious to man the destroyer grown in neat rows. In these rare woods jungle fowl abounded; and beautiful rose-coloured begonias, red and white balsams, tree ferns and orchids made lovely their dim recesses where the streams sang their songs of the ages, and ran down to turn turbines in the valleys far below.

The first tropical forest I ever knew was one of these reserves four thousand feet above sea-level, a very small oasis of less than twenty acres amid the unbounded desert of the tea. We went in to seek the monkeys, and we found them in a deep gully, where, waist-deep in wet undergrowth, we watched them moving high above us among the sunlit tree-tops, slowly feeding as they went.

High forest such as this has three levels of life, distinct and separate in almost every way, though the mighty trees live through all three levels. On and under the soil itself live the people of the ground floor, those who cannot or care not to climb, such as the deer and pigs, the porcupines, several kinds of birds, and far more kinds of insects, as well as most of the snakes and their chief prey the frogs, though there are tree snakes and tree frogs too. Life upon the ground floor of the forest is densely developed, and every footfall may carry death among that teeming population. Here, too, are to be found many lovely flowering plants, and a dozen or two of ground orchids flourish. Above this, midway between the dense undergrowth of the ground floor and the spreading tree-tops that roof it all, there is a more open space, where birds may fly freely, and where the branches are clothed in grey beards of lichen and hung with many sorts of parasite and epiphyte whose beauty excuses their indolence. There is not much food in this middle part, and it would seem to be used chiefly in two ways, as a medium of swift and fairly safe travel for the winged life, the butterflies, the bats, the marvellously tinted flocks of the orange minivets whose silver voices seem to trail light behind them as they romp through the dim-lit middle passages; and as a testing-ground where trees try out their strength in the hard battle that must be faced before effort may be relaxed and peace at length enjoyed. Down upon the ground floor each acre contains thousands of seedlings of the enormous parent trees whose bodies are the forest itself; and many hundreds of them succeed in pushing their heads up to the middle level, high above the head of any beast that might have devoured them, but still far below the roof, for there the hundreds must be reduced to tens, or even further, and their battle ceases only with the complete victory of those very few who live to be giants and live on for centuries, to found dynasties that tower as kings above the hopes of ordinary trees. This is a triumph of eugenics far more complete than any attained by the competition of animals or birds for mates, for only in the sunlight that shines upon the giants' heads can their seed be ripened, and of the unsuccessful none bear descendants. So above the middle region of travel and struggle there reigns a kind of peace, for there comes a level where trees have reached the full stature of their species and can race no longer to gain pride of place, to outshadow their rivals and starve them of sunlight. Ambition drives them upward no more, but is confined to pushing out on all sides so as to claim the largest available amount of light and air and rain. Trees whose great stems stand so far apart that they never knew each other in their youth meet in their prime, and, like kings, form agreements and compromises. War to the knife softens into rivalry for markets, and the struggle to slay becomes a competition for raw materials, where, deep in the earth, the outposts of the great trees' roots share among their tufted fibres every last particle of chemical value in the soil, keeping watch opposite to one another, but no longer fighting to kill. Their leaf-fall gives back all and more than they take, and through this eternal commerce the forest is enriched until at last it excites the cupidity of man, the spendthrift who uses in years the stores that millenniums have assembled.

Above the surface of the earth, and all through the middle levels, the kings of the jungle stand aloof, each encircled by the struggling masses of his people, born of his seed. But near the limits of their height they meet again, and share once among them every inch of space, for here, as among their roots, a balance of power is reached, and the widespread domes meet all along their marches in ordered rivalry whose victories lead not to extermination, but only to a rectification of the frontiers.

This is the richest part of the forest, and the hardest for man to know.

The upper surfaces of the domes are roof-gardens, carpeted thick with flowers whose nectar draws to the feast thousands of bees of many kinds, moths in battalions, and whole hordes of ants. Here grow the young leaves the caterpillars prey upon, and here, too, the young birds who prey upon the caterpillars, and the greater birds who prey upon the less, as well as those who feed in season upon the wealth of berries. Squirrels pass their lives among the fresh shoots, and monkeys love to sit waist-deep in foliage, while, with head and shoulders alone above the leaves, they look out over the countryside and shout to their friends in neighbouring trees. In the roof-gardens, where all rain is first-hand and there is no drip, where sunlight is pure and unfiltered by shade, where moving air ever renewed plays a great part in stimulating health, there grows an abundance of vegetable life more varied even than on the shady floor of the forest. For one variety of shade-loving orchid there are many kinds that love the tree-tops, and far more individuals of each kind; but this is not even suspected until the crown of a fallen tree be looked at carefully. All living beings in the roof-gardens hold tenure of the royal tree. Orchids and ferns, loranthus and lichens, they cling to their host and sub-let their leaves and snug corners to lesser tenants, lodgers and not householders, lizards and birds, bugs and spiders, scores of tribes of ants, and a thousand forms of fungi, until the royal dome becomes a kingdom, a thing a man might study all his life and yet not know to the full. For these royal trees are the jungle itself, the basis of its marvellous complexity, who draw from heaven and from earth their raw chemical elements, and transmute them to be issued in commerce through their merchants the insects and birds and beasts who eat of their products and the products of their tenants, and who in turn are eaten by the hunters, beast or insect or bird, who in time deliver them back to mother earth who bore them all. For each tree, and every living thing upon it, renders its final account, and squares its reckoning in the end by exchanging the body it returns to its mother for a share in her protean immortality.

By the edge of that wood a thing lay that was even older than the trees. It was a long stone, not moulded by hand, but shaped something like a boat. It was five or six feet through, and twenty or more in length, and it had grown to be an object of veneration to the coolies who worked amid the tea. When one smote upon its bows with a piece of rock, it boomed with a deep musical tone like that of some huge church bell, and the sound went echoing on through its solid mass. I have found flowers laid before it, and even cooked food, but whether it was a god I never learned.

Another thing was shown to me in that reserve by an ancient Tamil man who either remembered when the forest was first invaded by planters, or had known some one who did. He led me to the highest point in the wood, where it saddled the ridge, and told me that many years before an elephant road had run along the range from end to end of the valley. Agriculture had effaced it except where, in this small wood, it persisted as a shallow depression not yet overgrown by trees. This gave me my earliest inkling of the road-making powers of animals, and was the first time I suspected the existence before man appeared on the scene of something unconscious but yet so co-operative it might almost be termed organisation. Later on I found that all those mountain ranges had been carefully roaded by elephants ; scientifically it may even be said, if it be due to science, that certain wise principles seem common to all such roads. I do not mean to suggest that elephants laid their heads together and planned out a system of engineering, or, indeed, that any one elephant was aware that he or any other had any principles whatsoever, any more than a chaffinch who builds a masterpiece of a nest; nor do I wish to bring theology into the question, for such anthropomorphic treatment of gods and animals has marred most of the more famous tales both of beasts and of divinity, and I am more than anxious to steer clear of any suspicion of it. But seeing that road started me on the way to realising how animals, in like manner to human beings though in less degree, owe to their ancestors something more than the bodies they are born with. Individual families, for example, inherit landed property in the form of caves or dens, and whole races fall heir to territory improved and enhanced in value by being made easily penetrable and safer to travel through the discovery of fords and passes, water-holes and caves, and the provision of convenient roads leading to them. As time went on I travelled much by animals' roads, and my respect for their public works increased.

I have spoken of the planters as pioneers, but they were not the first men to know those forests, for although the Sinhalese had not conquered nature in those mountains within historical times, nor even left there prehistoric buildings, nevertheless there were large deposits of crystal flakes chipped by neolithic man. In the wood itself one could not find them, for leaf-mould covered the ground; but just outside, where roads and drains had been cut and holes dug to plant coffee and tea, they had come to the surface and were not uncommon, especially on the summits of round hillocks near water.

One of my neighbours, a grand old Highlander, had a nasty adventure in that timber reserve. He entered with a shot-gun in search of jungle fowl, and fired at one without perceiving that monkeys were hidden in a tree behind it, and greatly to his sorrow wounded one of the poor animals. He was moved by pity to go near and put it out of its pain, whereupon he was attacked by the whole tribe of frantic monkeys, and hardly managed to escape their just fury and win the open tea with torn clothes and gaiters bitten through. That is the only time I have heard of monkeys attacking man.

I suppose that little reserve is used up now, and I wonder whether the monkeys succeeded in finding new homes, or perished with the death of their royal trees. It is happiest to think that they, like the oppressed Israelites, may have found a Moses for their exodus, and marched by night, led by some old chieftain, while the babies clung to their mothers' necks, until at last they reached the promised land of the Government forest reserve in the Wilderness of the Peak beneath the cliffs of the holy mountain where Adam stood upon one foot for a thousand years before he was dethroned by the monkeys.

A MOUNTAIN VALLEY

In the hollow of the valley I can hear the mountain rill
Tumble headlong through the boulders, singing on from stone to stone;
And yellow-throated orioles the ringing forest fill
With melody, while high above I listen, all alone.

I can single out the voices of the minivets as well,
And blossom-headed parrots through the amber air have flown:
I can hear the hillside echo to the barbet's golden bell,
While high upon the mountain-side I ponder, all alone.

The silver-money chinkings of the love-birds never hush;
The robin's pretty flageolet from time to time is blown;
And cheerful friendly chatter among bulbuls in the bush
Never ends, but I am silent, on the mountain-side alone.

II. A HOLY MOUNTAIN

In the middle of the hills of Ceylon, now sacred to tea, there towers a mountain so famous that the literature of two thousand years in several languages would have to be searched if all references to it were to be assembled in one book. Hindus and Buddhists, Mahomedans and Eastern Christians alike revere the mountain as a holy place, and there is some evidence that the jungle people who came before all these did likewise. It is certain that the Peak was holy fifteen centuries ago, when the oldest Sinhalese literature that has survived was composed out of fragments and books already old and being forgotten; and it is almost as certain that it was holy a thousand years before that, when legends of Buddha attach to it, and when it became the refuge of some of the aboriginal inhabitants of Lanka who fled before the advance of the first Sinhalese invaders. Whether it was holy even earlier than that, in the days when the men of those mountains used chert and crystal flakes for their tools and weapons, there is nothing directly to say; but deposits of their antefacts lie upon so many of the lesser hills around the Peak that this too seems not unreasonable to suppose.

Holy in the past, at the present day it is so sacred that rich men, accustomed to wear European clothes and socks and boots, will toil barefooted up its rough and stony way to the shrine of the footprint upon the summit, more than seven thousand three hundred feet above the level of the ocean that can be seen as a glittering cord stretched along the horizon fifty miles away. To be High Priest of the Peak is one of the highest titles in the Buddhist hierarchy; but a more real holiness is shown by the fact that the girls of those castes whose women have from time immemorial made beauty their profession and its traffic their trade, will yield to no temptation while on pilgrimage to the Peak, not even while their feet have still many miles to go before attaining the foot-hills of the range from which the holy mountain springs. I have climbed it many a time when pilgrims by thousands wound up its rugged path by torchlight, singing as they went; I have camped with them in its sheltering caves; and with them I have kept vigil the long night through on the cold wind-swept summit, waiting for the rising sun to announce that the time has come to pray; for there is an element of sun-worship in all these religions that comes to the surface then, and the shouts of the multitude ring out like the cries of Hosanna in the Bible.

Among the pilgrims I have seen people of half a dozen races, with as many languages, and at least four distinct religions beside many sects, and I can testify to their reverence; for the East understands religion, whereas we of the West have made of it a form of warfare. There was no policeman there, and no one in authority at all, so far as I could learn; but the place was holy ground, and the tolerance of the pilgrims seemed a thing that might well have been studied by Western ecclesiastics with honour and amazement, perhaps even in shame. I mentioned this tolerance once to a bishop, and was told it was a sign of weakness of faith; persecution, I suppose, is a sign of strength.

Let this brief survey of the mountain's holiness from the dimmest past up to the present suffice without attempting to define what holiness may be, and whether subjective or otherwise; but of a use for this holiness in the future I have a word to say later. Where a force exists, it should be turned to good use. Near the foot of Adam's Peak engineers are busy now (1928) tapping the vast energies to be won from storing in a mountain valley the rain that falls so heavily in the Wilderness of the Peak. They talk in terms of hundreds of thousands of horse-power, and comparisons have even been made with the forces harnessed at Niagara; but I am thinking in terms of millions of man-power of reverence stored up through the ages, and will presently suggest a use it may be put to.

About a quarter of a century ago, after three pilgrimages to the Peak had whetted my appetite for its secrets, I set forth to spend some weeks in exploring its recesses more thoroughly. One of my aims was to identify the various places described by Ibn Batuta—the Arab traveller who rivalled Marco Polo—when he climbed the mountain in the middle of the fourteenth century of our era; but that aim I speedily abandoned. Some of the spots he mentioned were too easy to find, and some too impossible; and it was so utterly unimportant to identify any of them that I turned to more congenial quests, and spent my time in hunting for old inscribed rocks, and for the mysterious cavern in the lost valley where elephants go to die. This I failed to find, and since have wondered if the legend be one of those which seem to attach to particular geological formations, and are carried about the world by itinerant story-tellers until they grow naturalised in every clime, or perchance spring anew in human minds as freshly remembered things that lie so deep within us that they are common experience to the ancestors of all peoples. Such is the story of the secret passage from the castle on the crag, a tale which runs the length of Europe and through Turkey into Middle Asia to my knowledge; and another is the tale of the gigantic snake or dragon who lives in an undiscoverable cave beneath temples built on rocks. In the Nilgiris, too, there is a legend of a valley of death that none return from, and perhaps the story told by Hudson of the vale of death of the guanacos may be the South American version.

I found no gleaming pile of bones and ivory, though once the music played loud when I came upon a stone with the figure of an elephant carved upon it beside an incised picture of a pointing hand, with six fingers, but my search at least led me into many of the more hidden secrets of the Wilderness of the Peak. I climbed cliffs, and crept along high ledges where sub-alpine flowers rewarded me. I discovered caves long lost in forest but once the habitations of hermits; and from one group of these I followed an ancient way, long since abandoned and overgrown by the all-conquering trees, where flights of steps cut in the rocks led upward towards the sacred footprint. Inscriptions, too, I found, though none so old as I had hoped. Some were cut in stone where the surfaces of rocks were flat, and others were engraved upon links of the mighty chains that hung from the precipices, and once were the only way to climb them; but none of all of them dated earlier than the kings of the Polonnaruwan dynasties of about the twelfth century A.D.

I was told a tale of those chains. They hang over cliffs exposed to the full fury of the monsoon gales. Their links are formed like stirrups, and the pilgrims used, until steps were cut less than half a century ago, to climb them as a kind of swaying rope ladder. A whole family of Sinhalese villagers once set out on pilgrimage, children and their parents and the grandparents too; and when they came to the precipices and were all hanging on the long chain like a living rosary, a violent storm sprang up suddenly and the chain was swung fiercely from side to side. But they still hung on, though they dared not move in either direction, up or down. Then came a tremendous gust like the breath of an angry god, and the chain was swung so far to one side that it hung no longer over the pilgrim path, but clear above a frightful fall into a valley far below. And there, buffeted by the storm, unable to climb or to descend, the people hung while their strength endured, and then fell off, one by one, as fruits fall from a tree. First the old and the very young, then the women, and last of all the men; while the folk of their village who had been waiting for their own turn to climb upon the chain, and who had watched the whole tragedy while they cowered against the face of the angry mountain, saw in the end the strongest man of all, last of his race, leave hold and go spinning down to the tree-tops far below.

One inscription I found held some interest, for it served to confirm, so far as it went, the accuracy of the old monk who wrote that part of the Mahawansa—the Sinhalese people's remarkable history kept up at intervals for more than thirteen centuries—which gives a baffling and incomplete account of King Nissanka Malla in the twelfth century A.D. The historian says that Nissanka climbed the holy mountain, and this feat is recorded of only two or three out of some hundred and fifty kings who find mention. In a cave near the summit I found a little picture chiselled upon the rock wall, with a few words cut beside it in twelfth century script. It showed a man in an attitude of adoration with a rosary held in his joined hands, and the words read, "King Nissanka Malla worships the footprint on the rock."

Throughout these explorations my guide was an elderly Sinhalese man who had hunted for honey in those jungles. His name was Kiri Lamaya, or in English, 'milk baby.' He was unconscious that his grey beard made a joke of this, and I trust he did not become enlightened, for he was a real friend, and a most charming companion; after all, the name Suckling finds a place in English history. Kiri Lamaya had all the local legends and superstitions at his finger ends; and though his knowledge of the range did not extend far from the pilgrim path, his woodcraft sufficed to regain camp, however far we had wandered into the remoter parts of the wilderness. We climbed along ledges and hunted for caves, and some of the many we found had been inhabited by man, though more were the homes of nothing but bats or porcupines. Some caves we found could only be reached by the notches their former users had cut in the trunks of ancient rhododendrons which grew against the cliff, and in several of these there were inscriptions in Chinese characters cut into the rock and gilded. In this crumpled land of constant rain there is no end to the number of streams, and we explored many of them right up to their sources, but we failed to find the secret garden legend tells of, whose strange exotic trees drop blossoms that may be found floating in the cold torrent that bathes the feet of the cliffs of Ganguli Hela, an echo perhaps of the story of the Garden of Eden. In some of the rocks of the stream-beds captive boulders had ground deep pot-holes, and we found garnets in the sand that gathered there; but Kiri Lamaya told stories of the discovery of more valuable stones, a not unlikely thing, for the gem-bearing gravels of Ratnapura, city of jewels, whose sapphires and rubies, cat's-eyes and tourmalines have been famed for at least a thousand years, lie in valleys among the foot-hills of this range. In one stream-bed we found people who had been turned into stone as by Medusa, for some sin I have now forgotten; for this is a region where the miraculous is held to be as probable as the ordinary, and where the legends of all religions are interwoven; for the footprint on the rock, that which men go out into the wilderness to see, is sacred to them all. It is only a shallow depression in the rock, some two yards long, but to Buddhists it is the footprint of their founder, and they call the mountain simply Sri-pada, the sacred footprint. Hindus name it Siva's. Mahomedans of both sects call the mountain Father Adam's Hill; and though the modern name follows this in calling it Adam's Peak, Eastern Christians believe the mark to have been imprinted by the foot of St Thomas, who is peculiarly the apostle of India. But the place is almost overburdened with such names, and another common one, 'Samanala-kanda,' the hill of the god Saman, has given to butterflies their euphonious Sinhalese title *samanalaya*, for at certain times of the year when countless millions of butterflies stream out on migration they are supposed to be going on pilgrimage to end their short lives on the sacred mountain.

The Peak must be one of the vastest and most widely reverenced cathedrals of the human race; but the shrine itself is only a little tile roof raised upon four pillars, or it may be eight, open on all four sides to every wind that blows, and untended by any human being for months at a time when the rains are at their heaviest, and the only other building there in my time was a small mud hut of one room, which I was lent by the monk in charge.

Right to the very summit of the Peak the forest grows, and from the parapet wall itself one may pick blossoms from the tops of old wild rhododendrons and read in their mottled throats the name of god written in letters that all may read who will. Looking down from this wall one can see how for miles and miles on every side each fold of the hills and every valley is clothed in an ancient forest that has never known the axe, and is justly named the Wilderness of the Peak. The profusion of its beauty alone would inspire any sensitive being with a feeling of awe, and it may have been this unparalleled loveliness that led some man, who knows how many thousands of years ago, to name it holy.

I climbed up once when no pilgrims had travelled the road for several months of very wet weather, and had to crush my way through masses of begonias and balsams, and to tread upon pink orchids as I climbed, while the roofs of the shelters below the cliffs were clouded over with a mist of yellow calceolaria.

In the stillness of the evening, when no pilgrims are there, voices come up from this old forest, out from the depths of the valleys thousands of feet below, and from the slopes, and from the ridges of lesser hills that reach up in reverence like disciples beside their master.

Always there is the song of the streams which run hidden in their tunnels of trees festooned with orchids, dendrobium aureum, or macarthii; and often one may hear the cries of animals, the strident roar of leopards, the horn-like challenge of sambhur stags, the scream of eagles, the deep tones of the great black monkeys of the hills, and, more tremendous than any, the trumpeting of elephants. For the forest is full of life, though in its extreme density it is rare to see any living animal other than the squirrels and monkeys who move among the tree-tops; but their tracks and their voices betray the greater animals, and it was almost entirely due to their presence that we were able to explore at all.

This forest is a very wet one, and consequently very dense, and much of it is bound into an unbelievably impenetrable tangle by creeping bamboo, whose long tendrils, hard and thin as telegraph wire, form a mesh difficult for man to enter unless he can cut his way painfully yard by yard. To the elephants with their giant strength and weight it is a different matter. They live for the most part on wood pulp ground by their four huge teeth from the branches of trees, and this leads them to explore just as my different quests led me. All the time I was in the wilderness I found only one open space, high upon a col between two peaks, a fairyland of grass and flowers; but I had no difficulty in marching in any direction I desired, for the elephant roads ran everywhere. Man's roads pursue valleys for the most part, but the high roads made by elephants slant up the flanks of hills to gain the ridge as early as they may, and then travel along high ground as far as they possibly can. They are firm and of easy gradient to walk, though, walled as they are by the yielding but unbreakable netting of the bamboo, they may be perilous to use unless precautions be taken not to come unawares upon their makers, for to avoid a charge or even a startled stampede would be difficult, as although the bulk of an elephant is vast compared with that of a man, his road generally suffices only for men to proceed in single file. We went with caution, as though on the heels of great game. Kiri Lamaya took a further precaution, and I followed him to set his mind at peace, for he avoided all reference to elephants by name, lest they should hear and resent it: "The Great Ones," he called them, or "The Old Ones," or simply "They."

We were pursuing an elephant road one day through the very thickest undergrowth of all. What tracks there were led in the direction opposite to ours, so we felt sure we were not on an elephant's heels, though, of course, we might meet one; but all suddenly the road ended on a little flat place, and we found ourselves in an oval room walled round by unbroken bamboo. The floor was trodden perfectly flat and even, and the room was about the size of an ordinary drawing-room. Kiri Lamaya ventured the only explanation that seemed probable: he thought it might be a bridal chamber, the secret place of some gigantic love.

One is tempted to think that wherever a man may climb so may an elephant, for their immense footprints, smaller only than that on the mountain's top, are to be found upon the highest ridges, and on the summits of peaks hard to scale. It is only the encircling wall that holds them from measuring their feet with Buddha's, and I have little doubt that elephants stood there before ever men did, for chains are not needed upon the Maskeliya side.

Not only the elephants who made them, but all other animals of any size use the elephant roads, save only the monkeys, who have roads of their own through the trees and over the rocks. Without roads animals could not go in comfort at speed; where the roads cross valleys they indicate the fords, where ridges they reveal the passes. Probably they are of enormous antiquity, for such features as fords and passes change only with the waning of geological periods; also the standardisation of all such roads in their general system of avoiding valleys and pursuing ridges, and the similarity of their gradients, seem to reveal a very ancient craft now fixed in principles as scientific as elephants are likely to attain before man imprisons or slays the last of them. Doubtless man learned road-making from the elephants or from other great beasts when first he took the floor, for before the age of metals he could ill spare his precious stone tools to such blunting work as felling trees he did not wish to use. The flinty bamboos would soon dull the edge of a crystal knife, and I have little doubt that man in the Stone Age blessed the elephants even as Kiri Lamaya and I did. Did he too call them "THEY" as he hunted sambhur on the hills where I hunted inscriptions?

It has often been noticed by those who have hunted big game in forest lands how, after a few crashes, a startled animal's movements fall suddenly silent, and many a hunter has peered into the bushes expecting to find his quarry dead there, when in reality it is speeding along a game track half a mile away. I think animals always travel along roads for choice. They spread far and wide to seek for food, and comb out every inch of the forest, but when travelling on a journey, and especially when desirous of moving at once silently and with speed, they use roads just as we do.

One reads sometimes of impenetrable bush, where exploration is hampered or even for many years actually prevented by the impossibility of getting through fast enough to escape death by starvation or thirst; and it has struck me that the accounts I have read of this have all been written of countries east of Wallace's Line, where mammals are replaced by marsupials. New Guinea and the western parts of Tasmania are the cases I have in mind. It seems ludicrous that a country so small as Tasmania, inhabited by one of the most adventurous races in the world, should remain partially unexplored, and I cannot but wonder if it may be due to the lack of road-making animals. Marsupials are of earlier type than mammals, and may not yet have invented roads, for I feel sure that if a few wild elephants were loosed in one of the mountain ranges of New Guinea they would road the whole of their neighbourhood rapidly and thoroughly. Then, instead of cutting their way painfully yard by yard, explorers would be able to walk at normal speed; all fords and passes would be revealed to them, and in arid lands what water-holes there were would be centres from which roads would radiate as from Piccadilly Circus. No harm would be done to anyone, and to learn the rate at which even so slow a breeder as the elephant can multiply one has only to look up the calculation made by Darwin in the 'Origin of Species.' Long years after the rest of the world had forgotten what elephants looked like, the mountains of New Guinea might be a sanctuary for herds. One mistake only would have to be avoided. It would not do to put in a tusked variety, or contraband trade in ivory would soon end the experiment. Ceylon elephants very rarely have tusks, and are easily tamed.

There was one place that Kiri Lamaya feared more than he feared the Great Ones, and that was a sort of open cavern on the summit of one of the higher peaks. Nothing would induce him to enter it, for, he said, who enters there leaves sanity behind. Apparently there was some god who smote with madness those who invaded his privacy, one of the territorial wood gods, I fancy, though as a rule they are not malignant. Except for the god's invisible presence there was nothing there at all, and no sign of former human habitation. I entered, and, strange to say, I am one of the very few people I know who has been declared insane! It will be well to explain immediately that this was done by a Turkish medical board while I was a prisoner of war engaged in secret code correspondence with my own country. So perhaps that god had nothing to do with it, though surely my evidence would justify the building of a temple in his honour!

In one deep valley below the peak we came where leeches were as thick as the leaves that littered the floor, thicker than the hairs on an elephant's back. Every writer on Ceylon has told stories of these. Ibn Batuta mentions how in this very neighbourhood he was attacked by the " fierce leech," and I think it was Ribeira who told how they entered between the joints of the Portuguese officers' armour, though I should have thought armour alone would suffice to kill its wearer in the tropics. They were thick enough in that valley to be almost frightening. I relied upon boots and putties, but Kiri Lamaya, marching almost naked, carried the half of a lime fruit impaled upon a little stick, and with that light hammer tapped each leech that attacked him and left it squirming with its skin dried up by the astringent juice. And as we walked he told me the story of a man who came into trouble through leeches. He was a vederala, a village doctor of the Ayurvedic school of medicine, who went in search of wanderoo monkeys, whose fat he desired to render into a medicinal oil for the cure of swollen heads. In his benighted folly he pursued his chase on the lower slopes of the holy mountain, where he stalked his quarry and shot him. The monkey clung to the branch, and when he fell, hung in a high fork of the tree, and died there. The vederala wanted his fat very badly indeed, and began to climb the tree, but its branches were slippery with sodden moss, and his handhold failed, and he fell to the earth and lay there unable to rise, for his back was injured. Then the leeches came, looping along by ones, by tens, by hundreds, and at last in such myriads that his whole body was covered by their waving multitude, and all the blood was sucked out of his veins. The men who at last found him had to light torches with which to sweep the foul tribe of blood-congested creatures from his corpse before they could carry it away for burial. This was told to me as a true story, and I believe it, for imagination could scarce exaggerate the prodigious armies of leeches to be found in some of the deep wet valleys.

It was in a wet valley that I saw one night a very beautiful sight of the kind that gives rise to superstitious fear. It was too high above sea-level for there to be any termites, being actually a part of Adam's Peak itself, so the fallen twigs and branches lay where they fell until agents slower than white ants ultimately consumed them. The night that I slept there was very dark, and it poured with rain, but the whole floor of the forest was lit by the phosphorescence of some fungus that had invaded the dead branches. Each was a silvery green bar of shimmering light, and our faces shone as the faces of the dead.

In some of the valleys around the peak there are caverns among the boulders fallen from the cliffs above. I suppose that every one of them is the home of a family of porcupines, and several I entered had attached to the under sides of their sloping roofs small or large colonies of the esculent swift, the bird who builds from his own sputum the edible swallows' nests beloved of the Chinese. I examined many, and found their substance like gelatine or pale-coloured glue, but did not eat any.

Much has been written of the shadow of the Peak, which, as the sun rises, seems to be projected upon the air instead of lying upon the forest below as one's eyes expect. The shadow has even been photographed and reproduced in books. It is certainly a curious optical phenomenon, but it has lent itself to exaggerated description so often that I hesitate to speak of it. However, I once saw it from a point of view that has never been described, and which so impressed me that I called a friend out of bed to bear witness. I saw it from the Grand Oriental Hotel in Colombo, some fifty miles from the Peak, from a window over the porch of the old building. The morning was clear, and as it grew light I looked unto the hills whence cometh the help of the dweller in the tropics, and saw the battlements of the central range change from dead black to the amethystine translucency that heralds the birth of day. Then, with measurable movement, a beam of darkness crept from the top of Adam's Peak and stole up into the brightly coloured sky. It resembled the negative of a searchlight's beam, and in appearance was so odd and unexpected that I called to my witness that the Peak was smoking like a volcano. Then, as we both watched, I realised that it was the famous shadow of the Peak seen from below, and a moment later the sun rose directly behind the cone of the mountain until its gold was notched in the rim at 'six o'clock,' as we were taught to hold the foresight of a rifle on a bull's-eye.

Below Adam's Peak, on the *civilised* side, in the district of Maskeliya among the tea plantations, engineers are at work on the great hydro-electric scheme that is to turn this valley into a lake four thousand feet above sea-level, and thus create so enormous a quantity of power that, if ever their estimates are realised, and the water-power actually absorbed by industrial undertakings, the wealth of Ceylon will be vastly increased. This will bring some good, perhaps, as well as some evil; but one thing it appears to threaten is important, and that is the character of the holy mountain. It is difficult to yoke very, very ancient things with the newest improvements and preserve their old values; yet the power is there, and the wealth it promises draws men irresistibly to use it before it runs down to the sea. I would like to make a suggestion. The holiness is there too: why not use that as well? I would like to see the whole Wilderness of the Peak that still remains Crown property gazetted as a national park and game sanctuary, where none may hunt or shoot or trap or fish; where trees may not be felled, nor any orchids or other plants uprooted, nor any be purposely introduced. Within the protected area I would include the lake that within a few years will come to be in the valley of Maskeliya, for it will certainly grow to hold great numbers of fish, and will become the home of many water-fowl. It is already the policy of the Government to retain all forest above five thousand feet in elevation as a reserve for the conservation of rainfall, and nothing would be lost by carrying out the further proposal. Indeed, much would be gained, and a measure which may one day be upset if rainfall be found not to depend upon forests would be broadened and assured. Buddhists and Hindus between them number probably more than nine out of every ten pilgrims, and both religions enjoin respect for animal life as positive commandments in a way that sets an example to all other creeds. Ceylon has game sanctuaries in the Low Country, remote places where only an occasional official, a rare keeper, or a less rare poacher can enjoy what they preserve; but in the mountains there is no sanctuary, though nearly all the flora there, some of the mammals, many of the birds, and most of the butterflies, are different from their counterparts in the plains. And here the pilgrim path would enable all comers to enjoy what would belong to all. Coffee and tea have destroyed so much of the wonderful forest life of the mountain zone that it is more than time something was done to preserve and safeguard for ever all that remains unspoiled. The measure would be supported by public opinion so whole-heartedly that the work of wardens would be made easy, and, a great thing with rich governments, would cost little or nothing. As the lake fills, it may become a part of one of the most beautiful places upon earth, and not only that, but a treasure garden full of interest to the botanist, the naturalist, the specialist in rare forms of the teeming tropical life that in its entirety makes the kingdom of the jungle, from the great trees and the elephants to the smallest lichens and fungi and the microscopic things that live on them. The sanctuary might well become in time the last refuge of the Ceylon elephant, a distinct variety from the Indian. To the anthropologist and the student of religions it would be a place where he would seek for legends and folk-lore and the wisdom of ancient times. And it would marry together the ideals of modern England and ancient Lanka in a way few other measures could; for here, where the holy mountain will be mirrored in the water of the hydro-electric reservoir, wisdom can come full circle, and once more it can be remembered that a Sinhalese king, Buddhadasa, organised a national veterinary service fifteen centuries ago, and built hospitals for animals. Nor was he so much of an innovator as one might think, for one of his predecessors of centuries before proclaimed that the fish and all living things in the Bayawewa lake in his capital, Anuradhapura, should be freed from fear of men, thus perhaps being the first of men to form what we now call a game sanctuary.

If the step I venture to advocate be taken, it should be done at once, for otherwise vested interests in the fishing of the lake are certain to be formed.

WHERE THE ELEPHANTS DIE

THE eagles who soar in the mountain air
Have seen where the elephants die,
And know where their vast bones lie ;
Yes they know, but they do not care for a treasure of ivory.

Monkeys who peer through the tangled brush
Avoid the dim place of death,
Where the moon-flower weaves her wreath :
They stare, but they break not the hush as their little ones
hold their breath.

The wind that rides over the tossing trees
Pipes high in his sorrowful tone :
But he pipes for himself alone,
For he tells not a soul what he sees as he sweeps by the
place with a moan.

O elephants wandering far o'er the plain,
Or trumpeting high in the hills,
You may drink from the tumbling rills,
But you turn to the mountain again to seek for the valley
of pain.

III. TRUE FORESTERS

THERE is a man, I once was told, who, if he would but bestir himself, could write the best book ever written on the diseases of pineapples. There are many men who could write a better jungle book than has ever been written if only they could write at all; but I do not expect they will ever set out to do so until they have lost the knowledge that now is theirs. They and their tribe are called Gypsies by the English, because they still live the wandering life Gypsies try to live in game-preserving England; but the Sinhalese call them *Ahikuntakayo*, the Snake Charmers, for they are notable tamers of wild creatures, and are the folk who sometimes come into hotel courtyards to charm cobras or make monkeys dance before visitors. They call themselves KURAVAR, and what that means I know no more than the meaning of my own name. I fancy they can all speak Tamil, and many of them Sinhalese too, but the tongue they speak among themselves is Telugu or some dialect of it, and I believe they still consider South India their mother country, though all I have asked claim to have lived their whole lives in the Ceylon forests. There were Telugu dynasties in Lanka in the Middle Ages, and these folk may have come over in the wake of the invading armies; but they have little concern with courts, for they are true foresters, and like the deer and the mongooses, the leopard and bear cubs, the cobras and pythons and monkeys they catch and tame, are part of the natural fauna of the woods. By the authorities they are regarded as a criminal tribe, possibly with justice, although I had many dealings with their members at one time, and found no evidence of uncommon wickedness. Perhaps, like another of the nomad tribes of India, they may have a caste rule forbidding the commission of a crime within a certain distance—about thirty miles, I believe—of their camp. It is a wise rule, and if we and the other Great Powers could agree to some adaptation of it armaments might be reduced at once, and the acting of historical plays to be filmed become the principal function of the army. Kuravar do not settle in villages or live in houses, but travel about the jungle with a a few pack animals to carry their scanty belongings, and build their huts anew at each new home.

I had known these strange people as purveyors of entertainment for some years before chance first led me to make friends with one of them in the jungle.

It was in the month of May, and before either railways or motors had carried their blessings into the northern plains of Ceylon, that a friend drove me in his pony trap along a grass road through the forest some twenty miles south of the buried city where I earned my living by watching Tamil coolies dig up Buddhist monasteries their far-away ancestors had looted. My host was inspecting an irrigation work that has since caused thousands of acres of wild forest to disappear; some of it beneath the waters of a tank, in whose shallower bays the drowned trees still stand, gaunt and bleached white ghosts of the kings they were when first I knew them. Some of it went up in smoke and flames, slaying its multiform population, and has now grown to a dull uniformity of linear miles of aloes, the parents of manilla ropes, whose grey-spiked regiments stand to attention on the earth that nature refuses to leave bare. This was his work; and I, less harmfully, hoped to shoot a few wild fowl, or if very fortunate, a deer. I did shoot a few birds, and got a shock from it. While I was standing on the bund of a little village tank, bathed in an afterglow that set the sky afire, two whistling teal came flighting over me, and I dropped them into deep water a score of yards from the bund. A slim boy, brown and naked, slipped in to retrieve them for me, and the ripples of his swimming made harlequin patterns of blue and gold and scarlet where the mirror of the sky rocked in his wake. As he put his hand on one of the birds, a crocodile's black jaws broke through the colours and engulfed the other.

That had been the day before, and now we were fulfilling an appointment to meet a Sinhalese man who had promised to guide us to the 'Dam built by Devils,' an exact translation of our Devil's Dyke a ruined stone weir designed by some king of a thousand years before to turn the waters of a river into thirsty fields now lost—dam, fields, channel, houses, and even their names—in the forest that has covered up that ancient kingdom.

The guide met us by the roadside, near the camp of some black, rough-haired, untidy-looking people, very lean and ill-clothed, who all stared with animal wildness and human impudence combined, while one man stood expectantly behind our Sinhalese.

They were Kuravar. There were half a dozen bivouacs built of branches and talipot palm leaves, so light that a donkey could carry enough to house a family. Their entrances, that all faced away from the prevalent wind, looked like the arched mouths of caves, less high than the heads of their owners or my shoulders, and sloping away to nothing at the back. They seemed rather the dens of hunting animals than houses as we think of them ; but I suppose every Kuravan there had been born in one like these, and all their forefathers as far back as we like to imagine, for the Kuravan has no history. Happy is the nation that has no history, it has been said, and I think the Kuravar are happy when the authorities do not harry them too much. They had no possessions at all, it seemed, except the clothes they wore, a few zigzag silver bangles on the women's arms, plenty of silent watchful dogs of the kind we call pariahs, really a very ancient breed, whose points are depicted on some of the inscribed pillars recording royal grants of land as long ago as the days of King Arthur. The grants end with a protective curse, like that sometimes written in schoolboy's books, " May he who destroys this be reborn as a crow and a dog ! " and the dog whose picture follows is very like the hunting dogs of the jungle. The Kuravar had a few cooking pots, several donkeys, a couple of fawns, and their flat snake baskets. But this was wealth, if wealth be that which satisfies desire. If a rich man may be defined as one who is able to get all he wants so too is the man rich who wants nothing he cannot get. I fancy that a Kuravan's real wealth consists of dogs, snakes, and women. Dogs supply food, for they hunt everything there is, from the swift and wary sambhur to the eggs of lizards ; and it is claimed that the fine hunting dogs of the Kuravar sometimes tree leopards, and bay them until their masters can spear them. Snakes do not supply food so directly, though the Kuravar are reputed to eat non-poisonous kinds, and do not deny it; but they keep the Kuravar in clothes, for theirs is what officials term a money crop, something you do not eat but sell, so that you may buy knives, matches, and the like imported goods. The Kuravan does not often sell his snakes, for the market is easily glutted, but the sport they provide brings him the small income in cash he needs for the purchase of arrack for himself or ornaments for his women folk. So snakes and dogs are indispensable; and as for women, their uses are obvious. They cook the lizard eggs, and mend his clothes, and make the snake-stones. I do not think the Kuravar wash their clothes, but if they do, of course that would be another use for women. In a country where the morals of certain castes not more despised than the Kuravar have been compared with those of the chicken run, it is worthy of mention that Kuravar women keep to their own kind.

English Gypsies are said to eat hedgehogs, and their forest prototypes certainly eat porcupines, whose flesh, though too scented for my taste, is not at all bad.

Turning to the expectant man, our English-speaking Sinhalese, who acted as my friend's interpreter, said that he wished to charm snakes before us, and we gave leave for this to be done. He told us further that the cobra the man would display had only been caught on the previous day. The charming took place on the ground beside the trap we sat in, and was the usual performance. The Kuravan poured the snake out of the flat circular basket, whose shape as surely denotes a snake as a kennel does a dog; and after a prod or two the cobra sat up, displayed his hood, and made passes at the man, who dodged them. Then the charmer took between the finger and thumb of his right hand a little piece of the root of a plant I only know the Tamil name for, 'Vellei Errukkillei,' and holding this towards the snake, very slowly approached it nearer and nearer while the creature struck, or seemed to strike, at his hand. I noticed that he approached the head from above at a slope of about sixty degrees, and never stopped or hastened the slow downward and forward movement until in time his little bit of root reached the top of the cobra's head. Then, with his hand, he pushed its head down until the snake lay prone, when his fingers closed round its neck, his other hand took up its coils a few feet nearer the tail, and he slipped it back into the basket and put the lid on. We had both seen all this before, but the man deserved a rupee, and we paid it and were about to pass on when the man remarked to the Sinhalese that no white man could charm a snake. The Sinhalese himself of course, would have almost died sooner than have touched it, but he smiled. Up to then I had not spoken except in English, but I said at once that I would do with the snake what the charmer had done, and got down from the trap to make good my boast. For it was only a boast, and I had never touched a live snake in my life. The Kuravan opened his basket, poured out the snake, prodded it, and handed me the bit of root, and I copied very carefully what I had seen him do, with precisely the same result. The only time the man intervened was when the snake lay flat on the earth and I was about to grasp it. "Hold very firmly," he said, and I did so. Afterwards, when I got to know him, he told me the only difficult moment in seizing a cobra is when its hood is still partially expanded, for it may suddenly let this collapse and so loosen one's hand-hold.

This was the beginning of a friendship. Before all his people he pretended to make me free of his guild; mockingly I feared, for these things are not done so lightly, and yet I felt proud; and, indeed, he treated me afterwards as a friend and not as a mere fount of rupees. He rolled back my sleeve, and tied three threads in succession round my upper arm—a red one, a black, and a white,—and recited the while a sort of ritual naming me, my household, and my animals, for protection in language that recalled to me the words of the tenth commandment. He also presented me with a snake-stone, and promised to visit me some day in Anuradhapura.

When the Kuravan redeemed his promise and came to see me, he brought a cobra as a present. He said it was a female, and I took his word for it, and called the cryptogamous creature Mary. In the East one sometimes avoids the vulgarity of commerce by an exchange of gifts, and I gave an old coat to the man who gave me Mary. He handed me, too, a supply of pills to be taken when snakes bit me, red-brown and as big as peas. They looked like earth, and I never took one, and eventually lost them; but I wish now they had been analysed, only when one lives seventy miles from the railway station these things are not so easy to do.

I have talked snake by the hour with that Kuravan, and learned a great deal that was true as well as much that was otherwise. He did not believe that snakes cannot hear, and relied upon his pipe to keep them interested. I used to whistle myself, but one of the two greatest authorities on tropical snakes assures me that all snakes are completely deaf, even if a kerosene oil tin be banged above their head.

Mary lived for a long time, and grew quite tame; but I was a fool, and I lost her through my folly. To cure my servant of unreasonable fear of her, I kept Mary on my dining-table throughout a meal while he served it, and occasionally I asked her to sit up. Mary did not mind at all, but the next time I had to be away for a night she *escaped*, and never returned to me. I doubt if he actually killed her. More likely he just pushed the pane of glass off her box and let her go, or she may even have done it herself.

Quite early in our acquaintance the Kuravan told me that the cobra I first handled had its fangs drawn, and that all the cobras his people handled had suffered the same mutilation. About five months, he said, was as long as they cared to leave them without defanging anew. As for the public, if anyone demanded to see the fangs, all that was necessary was to catch one of the ordinary teeth in a loop of thread and show that, and they never knew the difference. I was surprised that men whose mastery of their art was so complete should require to take this precaution, but "What if I were drunk?" he asked me!

Mary's fangs grew again, I think, for one day a rat I had given her put up a fight, flew at Mary like a bull-dog, bit the edge of her hood, and cowed her into concealing her head in her own coils and pretending to be an ostrich. The victor sat up like a kangaroo in the corner of the box, and grinned his defiance; and I was about to release him in admiration for his pluck, when he fell over and died.

Two young Englishmen came to see the ruined city while Mary was still with me, and in the evening I asked them to my bungalow. Mary lived in a box in the verandah, and her only difficult feminine point was that she hated to be touched while still in her box, so I always used to allow her to walk out before I took her in my hands. She was just coming out nicely when the lamp blew out. We could hear Mary puffing softly, like a kettle beginning to boil, but we could not see her, and I did not care to feel for her. The two visitors fled into the garden, but they were brave enough to stay there and throw boxes of matches at my voice until one hit me, and I was able to light the lamp.

Many years after this I gained a side-light on what must at that time have been my reputation among my less scientific neighbours. I had long given up snake charming, but I heard it said in Sinhalese of another Briton who did so, "He has drunk so much electricity that snake bite cannot harm him, and if he were to marry it would kill the woman!"

Not long before the time I write of, a dweller in the hills had written to the newspapers a long account of a charming of snakes that had taken place near his bungalow. Correspondence ensued, and eventually a little booklet was published, and I obtained a copy; but to my hatefully agnostic mind the story presented several problems and held elements of doubt, so I consulted my Kuravan. He knew the story well. It was one of the successes of his tribe, and its hero was a cousin of sorts of his own; so I came to know the two halves of truth, which, like the two halves of an apple, fitted when placed together, though they were different, the one being complementary to the other. The rosier half was this, though to the Kuravan it seemed the greener, and it was the one that was printed. A charmer came to the door and asked to be allowed to catch some of the snakes which he said abounded near the bungalow, although its occupant might not have noticed any. Permission was granted, and they set out together, the charmer and the investigator, and not in the direction chosen by the charmer. The Kuravan piped like the Pied Piper, and soon drew a cobra forth from covert by the music of his magic flute; but, as he put out his hand to take hold of it, the snake bit him in the thumb so that two jets of blood appeared where the fangs had pierced. All this the writer of the pamphlet saw at close quarters, and vouched for personally. The Kuravan grew faint, but applied a snake-stone that clave to the punctures until all the poison was drawn from the wound, after which the man recovered and went his way, leaving behind him the magic stone, which was retained in the interests of science.

My Kuravan's half, never before printed, was different in several particulars. According to him, the charmer hid several snakes in various places so that he could make sure of passing one of them whichever way the chase developed. Then he took a long thorn and pricked his thumb twice near the root of the nail so deeply that it bled freely, after which he licked the blood off and went to the bungalow. Up to the moment when he was struck by the cobra the two halves of truth run parallel; but the charmer was not really bitten. When he made as though to seize the cobra, he provoked it to strike, and dodged its blow as a thing he did every day of his life; but he gave a cry, "I am bitten!" and seizing his *wounded* hand in the other, swiftly milked his thumb as though it were the udder of a cow, thus causing blood to spring from the thorn pricks. With the concrete evidence of his wound to his credit, the rest was easy, and my friend added wistfully that his cousin sold the snake-stone for ten rupees and a bottle of whisky.

Had he been really struck, I can only predict with certainty one thing he would have done. He would have preserved the life of the snake most carefully, for these men believe that snakes have power to undo the evil they have done, and he would have spent his last cunning in trying to win the pity of the snake so that it might suck back the poison it had injected.

I have never made snake-stones, but I know the recipe.

Take a portion of sambhur antler and char in red ashes until well calcined. Bury the product in black mud for twelve months, then dig it up again, wash it, break it into pieces of suitable size, and polish each of them with a stone. Finally, dish up with sauce, and get what you can for them.

But the men do actually believe there are genuine snake-stones to be found in the bed of a certain river in India, though I have not met a Kuravan who claims to have possessed one.

Charmers do not train snakes to do tricks, though there is no doubt that these creatures, like all others I have had except three only, soon react to kind treatment, and grow accustomed to be handled by some particular person in some particular way, though they remain conservative and impatient of innovation. The ordinary performance of a charmer, like my first lesson I have described, is based upon the ordinary reactions of the cobra. It cannot be done to snakes who do not raise their bodies off the ground, to sit up so to say; and no charmer I have known would touch a Russell's viper in the same light-hearted way, if at all. I found one imprisoned in a dry well once, an ancient well whose closely fitting stone slabs offered no crevices for climbing, so the snake lived there on frogs that were foolish enough to hop in. Like most ancient wells, this one had a projecting stone here and there left on alternate sides as footsteps, so I climbed down and captured the viper with a noose. I kept it for a long time, but never handled it, nor could I persuade any Kuravan to do so, though they offered to defang it and then tame it.

I suspected that cobras found it difficult to strike so as to hit an object brought slowly down at the proper angle. The Kuravar all said it was the root that prevented them, but I suspected otherwise, and at length proved my theory. My Kuravan never touched his snakes without having a bit of the root on his person, and sometimes he offered it to the snake to smell before commencing operations; otherwise he generally had a bit tucked under the bend of his knee while he squatted. Nevertheless I suspected magic, and determined to test the root's efficacy. Mary was docile, and aided my experiment. First of all I fashioned a bit of wood to resemble my magic root, tried it on Mary, and found she did not know the difference. Then I substituted an ordinary bit of match stick for the facsimile, and again Mary paid the same respect as always; so, after that, I boldly used the tip of my finger, and found it every bit as formidable. But, of course, Mary was a friendly snake, and although her docility had convinced me, it was not yet good enough evidence for others, so I awaited a favourable opportunity to carry the research further. It soon came. I was moving flower-pots in my verandah, and a wild cobra came out from among them on the cement floor, where I had him at a disadvantage, for the floor was slippery, and he only made ineffective S's of himself instead of gathering speed. My ophiological curiosity (in English, *damned folly*) came uppermost, and I tried on him the ordinary technique of the charmers, but without the root, so successfully that in a minute or two I had the cobra safely bottled in alcohol, which in those days, it may be of historical interest to record, was still obtainable by the poor.

I have pondered over this matter, and have wondered whether the snake's eyes, focussed upon a point above the level of their normal vision which is brought steadily nearer and nearer until they are obliged to squint, may suffer from strain, with that consequent partial paralysis of the optic nerve the earlier hypnotists sought to induce in their subjects by revolving mirrors and similar devices. I am not claiming to be more than a lay wonderer, and offer this suggestion very humbly. A phenomenon which appears superficially parallel is the so-called hypnotising of a hen, who is laid on the ground with a line drawn from her beak, and who remains still for several minutes. It occurs to me, however, that I have never tried whether the hen would stay there without the line being drawn at all. Nor have I tried merely putting my hand on the head of a strange cobra without going through the charmer's formalities of approach; and now I must wait until my children leave school before it can be done.

Among all the wild animals I have kept, the three exceptions who refused to react to kind treatment were one crocodile and two leopards. The crocodile was the only one I ever had, and was precisely eleven inches long when he came into my hands fresh from the egg. But out of the mouth of that babe proceeded a concentrated hatred of the universe that never abated. He never learned to love or even to tolerate me, hissed when I approached, snapped when I fed him, and after six months of constant care and unrequited affection that almost broke my heart, hissed, struggled, and bit when I set him free by night into a neighbour's pond; for it was too distasteful to emulate Mrs Bond and kill the creature one had already robbed of its freedom.

At different times I kept seven leopards, never more than two at a time, and of these, five were friendly and two were untouchable from the day they came to me until the day, some months later, when I fashioned a crate with a trap-door, lured them in, and packed them off to Hagenbeck, wondering to whom it would fall to let them out again. They were a brother and sister, so probably some strains among leopards are fiercer than others. My first pair, Hero and Leander, were the most lovable wild animals I ever knew. They would jump on my shoulders and kiss my ears, and it was their privilege to lap a little milk on the table while I had my tea. Boxing and wrestling with one another, they used to protrude the tips of their claws enough to be felt but not enough to hurt, but when playing with me, an inferior soft-skinned creature though friendly, they kept them safely sheathed in the beautiful pads that give them their silence and sureness of foot. Among many games, their favourite was to pretend I was a deer. They would make an elaborate stalk from bush to bush and from stone to stone, acting apparently in concert, until at the end they would rush me and pretend to grasp my legs; or perhaps they would dash past, striking and barely missing, and then suddenly and immediately calm down and stand indifferently gazing into the far distance as though they had second sight. They did not hunt at all except in fun, though they were free for hours every day and night, and could have found at least numbers of lizards and tortoises to catch if they had wanted to; but they did take possession of things belonging to me and refuse to give them up. Such articles as a boot or a cap they might annex, and it always meant a tussle before I could recover it, for they obviously believed in private ownership like all other wild creatures and like all children from a few months old onwards. And yet there are people who preach communism as though all nature did not deny it!

At that time I had two bears, and a jackal too, who was a mean-spirited beast right up to his tribal reputation; but of the bears, one, Rurik, was a fine character, and the other, Billy, perfectly good-natured.

All the five animals were in charge of a small boy, and every day they used to follow him for a walk as free and as tame as five terriers. I lived in a holy city that was mostly underground and covered with forest. It was a place of pilgrimage to Buddhists, and one day it happened that a number of pilgrims were visiting a ruined dagaba not far from my house at the same time that the animals were out for their constitutional. Like the majority of pilgrims, these came from far villages in the more populous part of Ceylon where bears are as rare as in England. They kneeled upon the pavement before the dagaba, heads on the stone, and tails about a foot higher, and worshipped the relic; and the scented blossoms they carried to lay upon the altar were by some of them placed for the moment upon the stones before them. All around them the scrub and high weeds were only cleared once a year, and to these civilised villagers it seemed a jungle. In this matter Rurik confirmed their judgment, for he walked along in front of the kneeling row and ate of the blossoms he found there. When the pilgrims yelled, Rurik barked, for he was not wanting in spirit, although so tame he was accustomed to canter behind my bicycle ; and when the boy heard the sounds of battle, he hastened to the voices, and the other animals thought it a game in which they were expected to run, so they hastened too. Of course, they outstripped the boy, and got there first, so the pilgrims saw the call for help uttered by their first foe answered by Hero and Leander and Billy and the jackal, and they turned and fled wildly. The boy reached me in a state between fear and laughter ; and the villagers must have made a tale worthy to rival that of the boys who jeered Elisha.

Rurik had but one joke, but he played it upon many people. In the mornings, when he lived in the verandah, tethered to a post by a long chain, it was his pleasure to loop the chain round and round the barrel of his body and strain against it as though he could not get another inch forward. When strangers came near to admire him, he pulled on his chain until he judged them to be within striking distance, and then whipped up his hind-legs, shook off the loops, and swiftly plunged forward the few feet thus gained. If he could, he clasped the stranger's legs in his stout curved arms, but he never really hurt anyone.

Bears and leopards differ much in character. I brought Rurik up from tiny babyhood, and fed him with the corner of my handkerchief dipped in milk before he could well walk, but he always went for me if I came upon him suddenly round a corner. As he touched me, he realised who it was and stopped, but his first instinct was to make attack his surest defence. On the other hand, if I surprised one of the leopards, it would sum up the situation in one lightning glance, and remain perfectly cool. Palpably its intelligence was far quicker than a bear's, as a hunting animal's should be.

When Rurik was found, newly born, in the hole his poor mother crawled into to die of gunshot after she had attacked some of my coolies who came clearing jungle too close to the nursery she had chosen, he was brought to me. He could not walk then, and if I put him down he would cry bitterly to be taken up again, so I know definitely he had received no outdoor education, not usually an easy thing to assert of forest-born animals. Following on that there were months of drought, and then one day it rained heavily, and the earth, which had been as iron, grew soft and sweet-scented. Rurik went into the garden and straightway dug into a termites' nest, a castellated hillock that had been of cement-like hardness ever since he could remember. With his long claws he bored into a main gallery, made a little hole, and then placed his rubbery and air-tight mouth upon it and sucked out termites exactly as wild bears do in the forest. On a smaller scale, the curious noise of his suction was precisely that made by a full-grown bear I had watched at this after being guided to the place by his sound from some distance off. This is recorded, as it seems to be an unusually complete instance of a skilled action being performed perfectly by a large animal at the very first attempt. As a contrast, a baby otter I had when new-born, and brought up in the same way as Rurik, could not or would not swim until I had thrown him into the water many times. He would stay on the other side of a stream I used to step across and weep and whistle till I threw him in again, when he would clamber out at once; but after a week or more he loved water better than land.

Only once did one of my foresters hurt me, a very tame young leopard brought up in a village hut, where I had bought him for six rupees that morning. When I got back, I released him in a dining-room with lights on, and I think the newness of everything frightened him, for he bit through my thumb and held on. I talked to him gently, and did not pull, and presently he let go and made friends, but I still carry a small scar.

Deer, monkeys, cats of many tribes, an armour-plated pangolin, and a host of other foresters must be passed over; but not the lorises. At night, when the light of the camp-fire flickers on the leaves, and far sounds come filtering through the tree-tops, the thin and ghostly cry of the loris is often heard, but though he is widely distributed and is not an uncommon beast, I have only once seen one at large, and that was in my own garden not many days after I had set free a she-loris because she ate her baby. I felt that captivity was too much for her and had better be ended. But I have heard the voices of scores of them; for they are very small, they live in the tree-tops, and they move very little until it grows dark enough for them to see, by which time it is too dark for them to be seen. Their figures resemble ours even more than monkeys do, for they have no tail, and on all but one of their fingers have delicate little nails like a baby's; the other has a claw. The Sinhalese of the forest recognise the likeness, and a not uncommon nickname for a very thin person is *unahapuluwa* or Loris. They creep slowly about rather in the way that chameleons do, but they can shoot out their long thin arms with startling rapidity. I have kept many lorises, for jungle men can usually find them, and they make gentle attractive pets. Only to keep them well they ought to have insect food, and that is tiresome to procure. One of mine lived for several months as a sort of Simon Stylites marooned upon a pair of antlers that hung in my dining-room. He could not climb up the bare wall, and he did not dare to risk the jump down, but I used to lift him off and place him on the table at meal times. The Sinhalese say that the loris, who weighs less than a rat, can kill the roosting peacock by flinging its long arms round his neck and biting to the brain. I doubt the truth of this, but doubt my doubts as well, and have some lingering suspicion it may be true, for I have seen one stalk and kill a sleeping sparrow in the manner described so surely and easily that he must have been used to hunting birds. For the most part mine lived upon insects, but they would hunt geckoes for themselves, and one I had came to a tragic end hunting in my verandah while I watched him. He pursued a tarantula, who could easily have avoided him, but did not seem to care to. The tarantula escaped, but not until he had bitten my loris in the hand, after which nothing seemed to help him, and within a few hours he died of cramp or paralysis. When my wild animals fell ill I used but one medicine to cure them, and the value of that was psychic rather than physical, for I used to drug them with laudanum in milk and warm water as much as I dared, or could get them to take, reasoning that as they all had perfect health to start with, and clean ancestry, though being wild they chafed more and were more rebellious against fate than domestic animals, if I could give them peace of mind they were likely to throw off any disease not necessarily fatal; and it generally worked.

A story of one of my lorises became known to some in Ceylon a generation ago. There was a very great lady, now gone to her rest: an extremely able woman, and much of a naturalist. All Governors' wives are great ladies, but this one was head and shoulders above the average, and the only blemish she had was a somewhat prominent moustache. She was a great friend of mine, and I gave her a loris. Some time afterwards it happened that the director of the museum and I were both guests at a fairly large dinner-party at Queen's House. He sat near the great lady, and I at the far end among small fry like assistant A.D.C.s. When the great lady spoke all other mouths were closed, and she chose to speak of lorises. The museum man, who was an F.R.S., was learned on deep-sea organisms but weak on lorises, and she sent her voice all the way down the long table to ask about mine; so the whole company listened while I told how one of mine used to sit upon the table and catch the moths that flew against the lamp-shade, and how he had sometimes climbed upon my shoulder and grabbed my moustache in mistake for a moth. Complete silence reigned while the great lady said very solemnly, "Mine never got as tame as that." I think she meant it as a joke. These dinner-parties bored her excessively, and I think she wanted to see the faces of the people she did not like as they tried to look as if they had not heard.

Like most nocturnal creatures, the loris has wonderfully large and beautiful eyes, and fiends who make quack-medicines sometimes tie the poor little things close to a hot fire so that those eyes may weep, and their tears be bottled and applied to the cure of an ailment which only people who would practise such an abominable act deserve to suffer from.

With the freedom I was able to give them, and in their natural climate, my animals were as happy as beasts may be who have lost their birthright. Rurik used to follow at my heels, and often accompanied me to my work among the ruins, where he would rummage about like a dog. Neptune, the otter, lived completely free always in my garden that had a stream running through it, and sometimes he went off for the whole day. The leopards used to have at least one good walk every day, free and unfettered; and the pangolin was accustomed to follow me to a termites' nest, where I would leave him free to burrow as he liked for half an hour at a time. Isabel, a pythoness, came back twice after she had been given her freedom, and in the end I had to take her out into the jungle, put her head into a hole, push her tail after it, and run so that she might lose her way and be compelled to accept the boon I offered her. But even thus I do not doubt that they would all have been happier if they had never known man; for, like retired colonels, they suffered from having no work to do. Sometimes it seems as though too much of our lives were devoted to the endless business of preparing meals and washing up after them; but it must not be forgotten that nearly the whole time of wild animals is spent in similar fashion. Even the buffalo, who eats that common commodity grass, has to spend a great deal of his time finding and consuming enough of it; and the flesh-eaters must often go tired and hungry to bed after hunting all day. So wild creatures have little leisure in which to grow weary of life, whereas the Zoo seems to me a sad place, where we make beasts share with us the burthens civilisation lays upon so many. It is partly their own fault perhaps for allowing one species to dominate all others; but it is sad, and I feel that if means could be devised to persuade all the animals we keep captive to earn their own livings they would be all the happier for it, and would probably live longer.

The ends of foresters are generally tragic, and Hero's death was particularly so. She had been used to the freedom of my one-storied bungalow, and I took her to stay in a large house where my bedroom was on the first floor with a balcony outside it. A towel was hung to dry on the balcony rail, and Hero made a toy of it, and I did not check her. But in an evil moment the towel slid from the rail as she tugged at it, and Hero, who had thought it made fast, fell down upon a cement floor below and broke her back. I kept her for a day, and she licked my hand like a dog as I tended her. Then I carried her into the garden, and stood back to shoot her; but she crawled toward me with her hind-legs trailing to ask me to help her, and tears were in my eyes when I put her out of her pain.

These animals, and the men who caught them for me, were true forest children, the men little more able than the animals to write a history of their doings; and they would all be patient of my ignorance if they could know what I have made of writing it in their stead.

BLIND DINGIRI

HIDE her in the thorny bine,
Poison berries overhead,
Safe, where living tendrils twine
Wreaths of scarlet for the dead.

Hide her where the vipers creep,
Patterned by the chequered shade,
Lidless eyes that never sleep
Watch for her the gods betrayed.

Lead her where the leopard cubs
Play as kittens lately born :
Guide her where the sambhur rubs
Velvet from his hardening horn.

IV. TANKS

In the Great War, when so many things had to be shrouded in mystery, some genius invented the name 'tanks' as a cloak for a new form of mobile artillery; because, it must be supposed, the name hid instead of revealing. With no reason of war to excuse it, the same thing happens in Ceylon, and the word tank there indicates not iron or cement cisterns, but the finest item of the ancient Sinhalese culture and the most beautiful feature of the country excepting only the mountain peaks and valleys.

I know a place where wooded hills that are the home of many bears thrust their long promontories far into a blue lake. In shallow bays between the woods families of pelicans cruise slowly, fishing as they go, their white bodies gleaming like a squadron of toy yachts. Waves break upon the shore, and crocodiles lie basking on the gravel there, or stretch themselves at length on little grassy mounds left by the receding water, where they lie with their mouths open wide like traps set ready for use. The trees that overhang the water are nesting-places for colonies of egrets, large and small; herons abound there, and several kinds of storks; and in shallow water the strange spoonbills run with their flat-tipped bills scooping up food like a boy with a shrimping net; plovers and sand-pipers run along the beach, and stilts with legs like red sealing-wax stand and whistle; and if one has fortune, rose-and-white flamingoes may be seen wading far out from land, sometimes in large flocks. Five kinds of kingfisher are common birds there, and I have seen another very rare one. White-headed fishing eagles call like clarionets from high trees where they watch for the shoals, and the chestnut-coloured kites mew as they hover hungrily along the margin of the lake. Once when I crossed in a boat and landed on the far side in a prairie of grass growing as high as my shoulders, a herd of wild buffaloes that I estimated to contain about eighty head rose up and stood in a curve of wondering faces hesitating whether to fight or fly. As the water sinks in the sou'-west monsoon, and the flats become carpeted with soft grass, the deer venture farther from the encircling woods, and herds of wild swine plough up acres of the new pasture in a night in search for food. This is the place to watch pea-fowl, for at the back of the lake they abound, and their loud cat-calls are the earliest herald of dawn.

To reach the village among the coco-nut palms below the bund on the deep side of the lake is a long walk, whether one goes by the north or by the south, for the water's edge measures more than thirty miles. Three sides of it are formed by natural rising ground, but the fourth was built by a king while England was still a Roman colony. From hill to hill he strung a bank more than three miles long and three hundred feet through at the base, and in it he built three great stone sluices, opposite to the deepest of which an ocean-going ship could even now lie at anchor and not touch bottom.

This is a tank; one of the largest kind, of whose class only a score or so exist in the island. The effigy of its builder stands on the bund. He has been deified, and a small temple of one room has been built to him; but his more lasting memorial pervades the forest for many miles to north and south, where he has been merged in the wood-god who reigns in that region now that the jungle tide has risen over the towns and villages that lived upon the bounty of his tank. The name of the king is known to history, though that of the older wood-god seems to be lost, for both are now united in the name of the tank itself, where, as god of the lake, they enter into the folklore and myths of half a hundred jungle hamlets. The hills above the tank are uninhabited, but they are still full of legends, not quite forgotten by the few people who roam them, though how long they will resist the age of petrol is uncertain.

To realise how such tanks came into being one must know something of the history of Lanka. The idea underlying the system was simple but very great. It was intended by the tank-building kings that none of the rain which fell in such abundance in the mountains should reach the sea without paying tribute to man on the way. In the middle of the southern half of Ceylon is a wide mountain zone, but to the east and north dry plains cover thousands of square miles, and at present are very sparsely populated. In the height of the monsoon, when armies of storm-swept clouds rush on day after day to match their strength against the hills, there is a line drawn by nature that the rains are unable to pass. It is as well defined as the line of trenches that severed Europe in the war, and infinitely more durable in defence. On one side thunder roars, rain pours down at a higher rate for the month than the rainfall of London for the whole of a very wet year, torrents grind deep grooves into the faces of the mountains, rice-fields brim over, tea and rubber thrust their roots deeper into the depleted soil, and dripping forests smell sweetly of growth and the urge of life. But on the other side of the line there is no shelter from the burning sun except where fugitive wisps of cloud sail so high above the baked plains, and are so spent after their battle with the hills, that their thin rain only reaches the earth to rise again in steam, and leaves behind it no more than the sweet scent of moistened clay for which the Sinhalese alone of all people I know have a special name. Streams dry up and become the roadways of thirsty animals; tanks dry up and leave in iron-hard mud their record of the last to drink from them; leaves fall from the forest trees and litter the ground, making noisy the passage of the smallest beast; large tracts of forest are deserted, and grow silent save for the rustling passage of the hot wind; and leopards gather on the flanks of the herds that are driven to concentrate near the larger tanks or along the banks of the few live rivers.

There are points where the line of demarcation of the two zones, the wet and the dry, is so narrow that within a mile one seems to pass into a new country; for the whole character of the forest alters, and in size, and kind, and distribution the trees differ completely from those one can still see behind one. The wild flowers take new forms and colours; different birds sing in the bushes; cultivation changes abruptly, and wealth ends. The line curves from sea to sea, and appears to be stable and unaffected by the operations of man, such as felling forests.

It is a curious fact that whereas the bulk of the population and most of the wealth have been found on the wet side of the line during the four centuries of European rule, it was exactly the opposite in the days before the power of Lanka declined. To make money one stays as a rule on the wet side, but to see the ruins of temples or monasteries, of palaces or engineering works, one must go to the dry side of the line.

Another fact, even more curious, has only recently been made quite plain by the government malariologist, perhaps without knowing it. He published in a report a little map of Ceylon with the prevalence of malarial infection in different districts shown upon it by varied shadings; the worse the malaria the blacker the map. Had I been making a map to show the prevalence of ancient inscriptions, the surest way perhaps to indicate the ancient density of population, my map would have hardly differed at all from his.

The theories of policy were widely different then and now. The rulers of old thought in terms of food-supply grown by their own people for their own needs. The whole of society was organised on that basis and the system of land tenure depended upon it. Hill streams were tapped and their water guided into the giant storage-tanks below, some of them four thousand acres in extent, and from those, channels ran on to other large tanks farther from the hills, and from them to others still more remote.

And below each great tank and each great channel were hundreds of little tanks, each the nucleus of a village; all, in the long-run, fed from the wet mountain zone. So gradually the ancient Sinhalese conquered all or nearly all of the plains that are now so empty of men; but for the hills where we grow tea and rubber they did not care; few ancient remains are to be found among them, and the forests we found there, and destroyed, were of immense age, and probably of true virgin growth.

The tank age endured for more than fifteen centuries, and then the jungle tide rose over it and all signs or memory of it became lost. It is now about one century since coffee planters attacked the forests of the hills. They have at last begun to conserve the soil, but in the early days of planting they lived upon nature's capital, and the humus laid in store by the leaf-fall of millions of years was flayed off by the rainfall of a few thousands of days when first the soil was denuded of its protecting forests, and carried down in spate into the sea; and now the older tea lives on fertilisers.

In time the jungle tide will swing once more, and then those who care for other things than wealth will wander back to the wet side of the monsoon line, and while elephants browse where tea is now plucked, antiquaries will unearth the ancient bungalows of the British period, or even of the Scottish which will lie beneath it, and classify the different kinds of bottles found among the ruins, and arrange them in museums. Having both planted tea *and* arranged the antiquities of a museum, I venture to prophesy that this picture will be realised in very much less than fifteen centuries, perhaps in one-fifth of that, or perhaps in one-tenth.

This comparison does not necessarily mean that the modern system is a failure, or that the ancient was better. The two ideals and their resultant forms of civilisation are so utterly different that no one should draw a comparison between them without special knowledge of both.

Village tanks are the centres not only of all human life in their vicinity, but of many other kinds. Cattle and dogs and buffaloes drink from them; the buffaloes with complete indifference, for crocodiles do not often dare even to attack their calves for fear that the whole courageous herd will rush in and trample them to death, the dogs more gingerly, and with infinite wariness. From tanks of hundreds of acres down to those that cover only four or five, each is a wonderful harbour of bird life, and even the smallest generally have a water-forest of lotus where flowers star the green as daisies star our lawns in England; or maybe they are the giant red lotus, like immense peonies, whose tangle of blue-green leaves are the home of the talkative jacana, the tank pheasant who runs on the tops of the floating plants, and of the gallinules, who live in deeply coloured families like purple poultry.

In the forest which covers the ancient kingdom, far from the sounds of men, one comes upon the bunds of tanks now utterly forgotten, where the banks have given way, and the beds become like natural glades for deer to graze in. Pigs find mud holes and wallow there, and wild buffaloes spend the heat of the day sunk in their pools with only the tips of their noses showing; and in the trees that ring them round monkeys love to linger, scattering the rinds of fruit upon the grass. In some parts, where abandonment is not so far back in time, no more than four or five centuries perhaps, the old fields have become park-lands whose open glades and clumps of trees are beloved of all the greater beasts and of pea-fowl. The largest herd I ever saw of wild elephants was browsing in one of these park-like glades: there were only sixteen of them, and three of these were babies, but their bulk seemed to fill the glade, and I walked amid the men of ancient times when man was not yet the dominant species fated to destroy the beauty of earth.

The men who built the tanks knew their business. I remember an engineer telling me how he had to take water from a channel fifty miles in length to supply the fields of the villages below. After he had made a level survey, he selected three spots where he cut into the bank a king had built about four hundred years after Christ, and in two of the three pits he dug he came upon the ruins of Sinhalese sluices; so they must have made their level surveys too, and plotted them to a yard with his. Another thing they knew was that a sluice should be slightly wider at the outlet than at the intake side.

I owned a boat once on a tank whose waters covered about three square miles. On one side a small town had risen from the ashes of a buried city, once the capital of Lanka; and on the other side forest came down to the water's edge, and wild elephants used to wade in and bathe. There is a railway now on the city side, and a hotel, and motor-omnibuses ply; but when first I knew the place it was as wild as a man could wish, and the haunt of thousands of water birds. When the whistling teal rose for their evening flight, the clouds of their flocks filled the air with their voices as they streamed across the afterglow in endless strings. Two ladies came from England to see the ruined city before trains had made it easy, and I took them out in my boat. "Are we likely to see a crocodile?" they inquired, and when I said "a hundred!" they smiled compassionately, but before we stopped counting we had reached two hundred: not in one place, of course, but during the hours of the afternoon.

In a shallow bay of that tank there stood a grove of dead trees whose roots had been drowned when the tank was restored twenty years before, and now their bark had all peeled off and they were bleached white by the sun. One does not see trees like that in the forest, for their wood is devoured by termites before they have been very long dead. Scores of black divers used to stay for an hour at a time with wings outstretched like coats of arms, while they sat on the branches of the dead trees and dried themselves; and egrets nested there, and dropped their precious white plumes into the water where young crocodiles waited for the young birds to learn to fly.

Not far away there was another tank, for the ancient city was a sort of inland Venice amid encircling tanks, and I used to go there evening after evening to shoot a teal for my larder. This was much smaller, and one could sit on the bank and watch the crocodiles fishing only a stone's-throw away. Sometimes a savage pair of jaws would be thrust out of the water almost vertically, and one saw them champ as they worked a big fish into position; but more often the hunters were hidden, and all one saw was the shoals of frightened fish that rushed out as the hungry snouts ploughed the mud, the big ones leaping high out of the water, and the little ones shooting out in silver spray like jets from the rose of a gardener's can. In the trees at the back a colony of weaver-birds had built their city overhanging the water. Dozens of their queer nests, like inverted stockings hung out to dry, were built together, visible a quarter of a mile away; and yet they survived, and built in the same place year after year; for the nests were mazes the birds of prey could not find their way into, and were too tough to be torn open; crocodiles guarded the bases of the trees from wild cats; and their only enemies in a land where boys do not collect eggs were tree snakes, to whom they probably paid tribute of their young so that the race might survive. I was charged by a wild buffalo there once, and had to climb a euphorbia, a tree like a monkey puzzle. For the wild came to the very doors of that small town on the buried city; and I once missed a leopard on the spot where an official's bungalow stands now and a monastery was built two thousand years before. It had killed a bull, and I sat in a tree above the kill with a lantern hung from a bough, for the night was wet and dark; but the leopard paid no regard to the lamp, so perhaps the idea that a camp-fire keeps wild beasts away may be groundless.

One day, near the end of the dry weather, I went to my favourite place to spend an hour watching the crocodiles, but not one appeared, and when I went to explore I found the mud scored with tracks running parallel, as though all the crocodiles in the tank had joined in migrating to deeper water. There were, I reckoned, the tracks of about thirty of them, and I never saw another in that tank until the rainy season had set in. I fancy migrations such as this are of frequent occurrence. As the smaller tanks shrink and dry, until from beautiful lakes they are reduced to wide ponds, from ponds to narrow moats along the contour of the bund, and so to a chain of pools, the crocodiles are crowded closer and closer together until at last they can bear each other's company no more. I sat by a village tank once that had reached the stage of being a moat about four hundred yards long. All the tanks in the neighbourhood had dried up completely, and their crocodiles were concentrated in this narrow creek, where they waited for the rains to come. Some lay out on the mud with mouths agape, others had wriggled half-way up the bund where they lay at all angles like stranded logs, a few had climbed on the trunk and branches of a fallen tree, and the rest floated on the surface of the pond. I counted one hundred and twenty-seven visible at one and the same time, and probably there were more hidden. It seemed a lot for the villagers to bear that six score crocodiles should live, love, and die in their only drinking water; but they took no steps to get rid of them, partly because gunpowder was expensive, but more owing to the apathy of people who have never known in all their lives what it is to be free from malaria. It was not from reluctance to kill, for there were keen hunters among them, and they did some contraband trade in meat.

When great personages visit the jungle they always shoot crocodiles. It is easy, and the cable looks well: "Man-eating crocodile killed." Are there such things, I wonder, as crocodiles who would not eat man if they could get him; a fat child, for example? I doubt it, and think 'man-eating crocodile,' like apple-eating boy, denotes opportunity and not a degree of turpitude. I once killed nine in a morning, and even now that my feelings have drawn nearer to Buddha's I cannot feel very penitent, though I would not repeat it, for it is not a high form of sport. Only twice have I killed crocodiles in a way at all sporting, for sport must contain an element of risk, even if it is only the risk of being found out! In one case the risk was mine, and in the other it fell to a Mahomedan coolie, and he shall have preference. It was drawing towards evening, and I sat by the ruins of a shrine on the high bund of a tank with a shot-gun in my hand, hoping that green pigeons would fly over me, for in those days of happy poverty I relied on my gun to feed myself. In my pocket, as always, lay two ball cartridges, for one never knew what might come along, and it was a fixed rule to carry them.

In the tank below me some men were bathing, and one had swum out beyond the rest; but suddenly he turned with a cry, and raced with splashing over-arm strokes to the foot of the bund where I sat. "*Crocodile!*" yelled his friends, and I saw a crocodile swimming on the surface apparently in pursuit of the splashing man. By the time I had loaded with ball it was almost up to his legs, so I stood up to get the additional height to enable me to fire over and not into the man's back. It was a lucky shot, but a shot has to be lucky for someone! I fired over the man and hit the crocodile in the head, whereupon it sank and was no more seen. The man was out of breath, but he had a great adventure to tell for the rest of his life, and I a small one.

The other adventure was my very own, shared only by the crocodile. Once more I was looking for green pigeons, this time in the bed of a breached and abandoned tank where trees had grown in scattered groups like an old orchard; they were wild bauhineas for the most part, whose wood is used by the Veddhas for making fire by stick friction; but along the line of the bund towered a row of huge giants of another species whose roots love water. Two small boys hung by my heels, to carry my game and share the sport. Their home tank had dried up, and now the whole population of their village, a score of souls, had lived for several weeks beside a pool in the bed of this old tank, where they waited for the rains to render their hamlet habitable once more. Soon another boy joined us, and to me he said, " Would you like to shoot a crocodile ? " " Yes," said I, and he led me to look for it. He took me to the bund where the orchard of wild fruit ended and the great trees stood as a rampart on the edge of the forest, and to one of these giants he pointed and said, " It is in that cave." The tree leaned, for a gale had blown it at some time against the trees behind. It could not fall, for they propped it up, but its roots had torn up the top of the bank on which it grew in a pad, and beneath them was a cave, as the boy not unjustly called the wide low crack that had opened in the earth. I think it was about twenty feet long, and I know it was not high enough for a man to crawl into on hands and knees; but it was high enough for a short-legged crocodile to do so, and it seemed to go a long way in. I was young, though not so young as that boy. Perhaps I was more foolish. Anyhow, I fulfilled my contract to hunt a crocodile, and went in lying flat on my stomach and pushing with my toes. It smelt more than earthy, and was very dark, but soon a gleam of light was reflected by the eye of the poor beast who had hidden there to await the rains that were to release him and make all happy once more in his tank as in the homes of the marooned villagers. It proved easy to kill him. Indeed I could not miss, for I could have poked him with the gun ; so it was fortunate he died without lashing out even once ; for crocodiles are marvellously retentive of life, and the most ghastly sight I ever saw was a crocodile a man had shot, dead as he thought, and half-skinned, starting off with flapping hide to try to reach water.

This one died with no struggle, and I hastened out again, dusty, half-deafened, thirsty, and for some obscure reason shaken with laughter. But now I had as good a story as the Mahomedan coolie.

Beside tanks one sometimes finds stones with cobras carved upon them. The body of the snake is treated conventionally, arranged in plump curls, and there are generally three, five, or seven heads with their hoods raised. Cobras with many heads are common motives in Sinhalese sculpture, and are called Nagas, a word that means cobra in many of India's languages. But in the beginning of Sinhalese literature people called Nagas find frequent mention, and had lent their name to a part of Lanka at least as early as the time of Ptolemy, for he gives them a place on his map. This is but one of the frequent glimpses we get in the jungle of tribes that were old when the Sinhalese were new ; for, like the submerged religions still known and practised by the jungle folk who call themselves Buddhist, there are submerged traces of pre-Buddhist culture of many kinds that should be collected before it is too late.

Some word must be said on the strategical aspect of tanks, for it almost certainly influenced Sinhalese history profoundly. A city encircled by tanks could not easily be invested, for the perimeter to be covered by the investing force would become too extended, and supplies would get through ; but this is not the point I wish to discuss.

The ingredients of instability were these, if such a word may be used of a civilisation which endured so long.

The kings were polygamous, and married the daughters of rajas of neighbouring kingdoms in South India. It often happened, therefore, that a king had many sons, all of whom might be ambitious.

All land was held on service tenure, and in that feudal system the overlord could call upon his tenants to follow him in war. Ambitious princes therefore could command a following irrespective of the justice of their cause, or of its chance of success.

There was thus every temptation to wage civil war, and it might be said without injustice that civil war was the rule rather than the exception after the termination of any long and successful reign. When a prince was defeated he fled to India, where he had relatives, and there either awaited another chance of recovering his lost position, or raised an army of mercenaries, whom he bribed with promises of loot, and invaded the kingdom he aspired to govern.

This is where the importance of the tank system comes to be linked with the history of Lanka's decline and fall. Possibly the Sinhalese may have respected the channels so long as their wars were strictly among themselves, but when Indian mercenaries came in, led by some Cholan or Pandiyan chief who had heard of the wealth of the temples and monasteries of a creed alien to him, naturally they cared but to injure their opponents as quickly and as thoroughly as they could.

The records are written by monks who knew little of the tactics of war and did not describe them, but they did not spare their bitter complaints of the looting and destruction of the monasteries; and from the enormous repairs found necessary after each period of civil war, and recorded in the list of each great reforming king's deeds as second, in the eyes of the monk historians, to his pious gifts to monasteries, we can tell that tanks and channels suffered terrible damage in war. Their bunds must have been cut as an ordinary tactic, or as a reprisal, frequently, and with disastrous results. Anuradhapura, the old capital, derived its water supply from the enormous tank Kalawewa, distant by channel more than fifty miles from the town.

Into one large tank that spread for more than six hundred acres against the western quarter of the town, the water from Kalawewa first ran; then from that to another smaller tank, but yet nearly a mile across, in the middle of the city, right among the monasteries and temples; and from that again to smaller tanks and ponds and pools for bathing, for washing clothes, for drinking, or for growing lotus blooms. The very life of the city was bound up with this supply of water brought from so far away, so what could be easier and more effective than to cut the channel somewhere along its serpentine course of three-and-fifty miles? Modern soldiers would not hesitate to do so, and we have no reason to suppose that those of ancient times were more merciful, or less sagacious. In the result fields would be thrown out of cultivation, and standing crops ruined; clean running water, not only throughout the city but over wide areas, would dry rapidly under the tropical sun into a string of pools; millions of small fishes would be left to perish of drought, and millions more would be captured by birds where they still fought for life in water all too shallow for them; and mosquitoes would multiply at an appalling rate.

The best way to combat malaria is to drain pools where the larvæ of the anopheles mosquitoes can live, and the second best way, where for some reason the pools cannot be drained or filled in, is to introduce small fish, who, multiplying quickly, feed upon the larvæ and control them, preventing their increase. War among the tanks reversed both these beneficial measures rapidly and completely, and we cannot doubt that war was almost certainly followed by an epidemic of malaria. That is why the Sinhalese eventually became too enfeebled to keep up the mighty works their ancestors had built, for doctors can measure, almost with precision, the percentage of energy that is lost by malarial infection.

It explains, too, why the map made by the malariologist should so closely follow the map that might be made of the known inscriptions and ruined sites.

It explains why the jungle tide has risen and submerged that ancient kingdom so completely.

Malaria is so universal in the jungle villages of the old kingdom that I never knew a person who lived there and had not had it, not even a child. A friend of mine who once accompanied me through the country I have tried to describe was a doctor, and he examined every child in each hamlet we came to. I talked to the kiddies and fed them with biscuits, while he felt their distended little tummies, and among them all found not a single child who had not an enlarged spleen, the sure sign of chronic malaria.

So the kingdom went back to the woods, and one may wander for years among ruins and find no end to them. Must one be ranked as opposed to civilisation if one prefers the dry and thinly populated side of the monsoon's frontier to the prosperous and wet one?

That is a question I find it impossible to answer without first settling what the word *civilisation* means.

THE GREEN PIGEON

O Flutterer of green, amid green leaves,
Is it joy, pure joy, makes you whistle like a boy,
Knowing half a tune he never quite achieves ?

O Learner of a wistful melody,
I can hear your quaint refrain, lilting down and up again,
Where you crouch among the leaves half-hid from me.

O Teacher of a woodland harmony,
I can see your colours blend with the leaves, and without end
Through my heart there runs the tune you taught to me.

V. WILD BEASTS AND BURIED CITIES

A FRIEND of mine in the jungle owned a stalking buffalo, the most intelligent bovine animal I have known. Even in a land where buffaloes are universally used on the farm, and perform practically all the work involved in rice-growing; where they are driven in carts, and trained as pack animals, it is rare to find a stalking buffalo. The owner of this one told me that very few buffaloes could be persuaded to do the job efficiently. In all jungle villages the buffaloes share the lives of the human beings almost as intimately as the dogs do, and their woolly calves hang around the doors among the children and hens; so they become very tame, although they are in no particular distinguishable from their wild brethren with whom they interbreed freely. The first wild buffalo I ever killed was shot at the earnest desire of the villagers whose cows he had taken possession of, driving away and wounding their lawful spouses, the tame bulls.

There was no question of stalking him, for he was out with the cows he had won in the middle of a wide expanse of grass and rushes, two miles across, once the bed of a great storage tank. I walked right up to him and fired two shots while he stood like a king, head up and eye meeting mine, and never showed that he had been hit until he died. I have not seen a nobler animal, and I think the villagers would have done well to let him sire their calves in peace.

Once I made a long journey in rope-soled shoes; and when their tips had worn through, and the tips of my toes gone after them, so that I could walk no more, I rode for one whole day on buffalo-back. The saddle was a sack and the girths coir string, and our pace did not exceed three miles an hour; but the journey was not a comfortable one, for that buffalo's skin seemed to be a misfit, and slid so freely round the barrel of his strong body that the sack and I could acquire a list of thirty degrees, while still retaining our hold upon the same portion of skin.

I learned the few words of that animal's vocabulary, and none could have been tamer or more free with rough comradeship than my mount.

But the stalking buffalo was equally tame and more intelligent. His owner was a short dark man, a Veddha by race, and a true son of the jungle. Even the best Sinhalese trackers have a word of respect for the Veddha, whose high caste they allow, and whose race they admit to be older than their own. This man, Undiya was the head of his clan, the Clan of the Bow, and in his own jungle counted as a kind of chief. We became close friends, for his advantages had not made him proud, and, like other instances of symbiosis, we were useful to one another; for if in the provision of hardware I could lead, he was more deeply learned in the mysteries of woodcraft than any one I ever knew, even Kapurala. And this was not surprising, for he told me that his people had only settled down to live in villages at all during the generation preceding his, and even in his lifetime they had changed several times from one range of jungle to another, and still, when I knew them, were more at home in caves than in houses. Each time they moved they chose some small abandoned tank, and patched up its bund so that a pool could accumulate for a water supply. They even had a field or two, but more of their wants were still supplied by hunting than by agriculture, and they valued their dogs nearly as much as their cattle. Generally we met in the woods, far from the dwellings of man, but I have visited their hamlet, where the houses are still of temporary character, built of boughs with the leaves on, quite unlike the earth-built huts the jungle Sinhalese live in.

Of all kinds of forest-lore this man was a master, and it was he who taught me how to make fire by rubbing sticks. Many years afterwards I asked some young Veddhas if they could do this, and all but one said they had never seen it. One, however, said he had seen it done, though he could not do it himself; but when I asked him where he had witnessed the practice, he replied, "Here! I saw you do it when I was a little boy." So the art seems to be dying out, for that must have been when Undiya, his grandfather, taught me in the very cave where we were then camped.

It was when it came to stalking that Undiya's superiority over me rose highest. He could not see better than I could, but could interpret far better what he saw, and looking into a thicket would tell from a few square inches of a motionless animal's hide what kind it was, and generally the sex as well, where all I saw was skin. At hearing we were barely equal, for I held a slight superiority. When it came to recognising a scent he could make a good guess, whereas I might as well have been the rich Sinhalese man who once came to buy land at a sale I was conducting wearing a pink celluloid artificial nose on his brown face which lacked one. But it was in the sense of touch all over the body that makes or mars a tracker that he was supremely excellent. The test of good stalking is speed. Almost any one can learn to move silently at two yards a minute, but when I tried to keep up with Undiya, leaves would rustle and twigs would crack until everything for a furlong around us was standing on tiptoe with ears cocked and nose twitching, ready to fly like a loosed spring at any moment. At my own speed, Undiya following, I once crept up-wind to within a few yards of a wild buffalo cow who had just calved and was licking her baby. We went through pretty dense scrub to do it, thorny and with nothing stout enough to climb in case of trouble; but we got there, and we got back again without the wild mother ever knowing her secret had been discovered by a man. It was not a very fair thing to do, for if she had discovered me, I should have been compelled to choose forthwith between murder and suicide, for she would have charged instantly, and never let up hunting me relentlessly until one of us was dead. It was done as a test: to prove to myself that I could stalk; and I was not out to shoot at all, for I had ceased to kill for sport, and would not have even coveted her husband's head had I seen him. Undiya could not have gone more quietly by himself, but he could have gone there and back while I went half-way there.

The stalking buffalo is a device that does away with the necessity for silent movement. When we went out, Undiya held its tail with one hand, and a guiding rope with the other, and off we went like Young Lochinvar through the most difficult and tangled jungle we could find. Undiya wore nothing but a foot of calico, and he was a very short man; but the noise of my boots and of the hard branches scraping against my clothes did not matter in the least, for the buffalo's hoofs and the thorns against his tough hide made similar sounds, and masked my noise to the listening people of the woods. Some of the ground we traversed was very wet, and the buffalo took delight in plunging through mud, or tearing his way through swampy thorn brakes with a noise that could be heard for a quarter of a mile. Nevertheless we came upon several sambhur, one muntjac, and four or five families of spotted deer, most wary of wild beasts, and they paid no attention at all. When we hove into view they generally turned their heads in our direction, but when they had confirmed the news their ears had already given them, they went on with their own business, and gave not another thought to the buffalo, or to the men who crouched behind his bulky form. Of course we had to avoid giving them our scent, and in this difficult matter Undiya displayed much skill in the way he managed to quarter the ground so as to show me everything in it without disturbing them. Had I been hunting for sport I could have killed the first deer we saw, and then probably would not have seen another that day. We saw no dangerous animals, but Undiya said it was as easy to approach elephants or bears as we had found it was with deer; leopards, however, might excite the buffalo.

These memories of buffaloes have taken some time to write, and Undiya and I spent the best part of a day at the fascinating pastime of seeing without being seen, a most back-breaking day; but where the experience links up with the title of this paper only becomes apparent when I mention that we spent that day without straying beyond the limits of a monastery whose rock-cut inscriptions show it to have endured from about the end of the third century B.C. to about the beginning of the thirteenth century A.D., when calamity fell upon it. In the middle of projected new works its people fled, leaving images unfinished, and stones in the quarries half-carved. Their hopes are shown by the labours they had set out to perform, but there is no sign of subsequent human occupation from that day seven centuries ago to this, except that an exotic flowering shrub grows before one of the caves and seems to indicate that a hermit sojourned there within the lifetime of the bush, something less than fifty years.

I do not mean that for the whole of the day we were within the four walls that included the buildings, though we were for a good deal of the time; but our buffalo preferred low-lying swampy land, so I think we must have traversed the lotus ponds, and the bathing pools, the pond where the semi-tame, semi-sacred fish swarmed, and perhaps a good deal of the outer demesne as well. Where monks had tethered their cart-bulls, deer fed unfettered, bears drank where holy men had bathed, the leopardess had cubs where the rule of celibates had excluded women as sternly as on Mount Athos, and elephants' gigantic droppings soiled the precincts of shrines where scented blossoms had for a thousand years been laid reverently before the statues of Buddha, the Wise Man, founder of the faith that had called the monastery into being.

This is a thing that may so easily happen in Ceylon, where a kingdom lies hidden in a forest, that it only calls for comment when for an hour one is impelled to stand aside from the life one is living to take thought of the strangeness of things, and of how they come full circle when the civilisation that destroyed the wonderful community of the trees and animals lives its last day, and the unweary tide of the jungle flows over the empty temples and hides their ruins with its counterpane of flowers.

I once lost the reigning Governor of Ceylon. This disaster was not gazetted, for I found him again, but for the most of a day his wife was very anxious, and her agitation was conveyed to various minor officials, and spread contagiously until Veddhas were called upon to track down His Majesty's representative. They did not run their quarry to earth, for I found him first.

It all happened this way. The Governor wished to visit a certain ruined temple where some remarkable frescoes still retained their colours after six centuries of neglect, and he asked me to take him to see them. There were two ways to choose from : one led through the forest along a footpath, and the other crossed beautiful park lands where open glades alternated with woods, and where we were likely to see something of wild life. By cutting across these, the walk could be reduced to about three miles each way, and was more out of the ordinary run. In the event it proved to be very much out of the common routine of a Governor's life, for I mistook one cattle track for another, where all looked much alike, and went a shade too far to the north, thus failing to cut into the forest footpath which led to the ruin but no farther. On we went, and when we had been a couple of hours afoot I knew we had missed the frescoes, lost our way, and were heading for very wild uninhabited country. There were plenty of game paths, and they bore the fresh imprints of buffaloes that might or might not be wild, and of elephant, leopard, bear, and several kinds of deer that certainly were ; also there were damp hollows where wild pigs had dug, and in the trees above us endless tribes of monkeys moved. So the Governor had many interests added to what must normally prove a tedious career. But it was hot, he was more than sixty years old, and he became very tired and thirsty.

Once, twice, and a dozen times I climbed trees to try and catch sight of some landmark; but those who have not tried to do this may not realise what an exceedingly difficult thing it is to do. On the actual floor of the forest, where the jungle-fowl and great lizards run, one can see a good long way, and trackers drawing nigh to a wounded animal often put their faces close to the ground to look for his feet, which may be visible though his whole body be hidden. Above that space there comes a blind level where the shrubs bear leaves, and then comes the open region of the large branches, where forest eagle-owls fly through dim corridors, and it is seeing how open this mid level is that lures one to climb trees for a distant view. But the hope is illusion, and the obscurity of the shrubs is exchanged only for the equally baffling blindness of a world of small branches, where the outer ramifications of the great boughs carry their masses of leaves. Unless one can find a tree that rises above the rest—as a spire above a city,—it is not of much use to climb it, for the actual tip-top cannot be reached, and any lower position is valueless. If one can find such a tree, probably its lofty stem will prove unscaleable. So, after a while, I gave up climbing trees, and we strove to keep direction by the aid of the wind—no easy thing to do when sunk in the bottom of a sea of forest. The sun gives little help in the middle of the day in the tropics, and I had not brought a compass.

At last the Governor grew so thirsty that I had to climb one more tree to get him berries to eat. There were very few I could reach, and I gave them all to him. "Weren't those delicious, Miles!" he exclaimed as he finished the last of them, and the most perfect A.D.C. in Asia replied, with a desiccated tongue, "Yes, sir, quite delicious."

That Governor was a great gentleman. When at last I found the way out, and we stumbled wearily along to the door of the circuit bungalow he occupied, I began to voice my apology; but he cut me short with, "I have enjoyed my walk, and you must come to dinner."

I do not know how many miles we walked, but I do know that we never passed outside the limits of the buried city. The places where the animals' footprints were held in record by the mud, hard as plaster casts and insoluble until next rains, had once been public baths, reservoirs for washermen to beat clothes in, ornamental ponds, or pools where lotus blooms were grown for temples. The mounds where grew the trees I chose to climb were compact of tile and brick, and their earth had once been beams and rafters; where the streamlets had run after heavy rain the dry sand was full of broken pottery, and the game paths we walked cut through ridges whose soil was red with bricks that once were walls.

Not that day, but in those same woods, I went out to shoot a jungle-cock, and was lured into the thickets by a bird who kept calling and moving just out of my sight. When at last I shot him, and went to pick him up, I discovered the ruins of a lovely pond built of stone slabs carved to resemble the open flower of a lotus, and strangely enough what appears to be this very pond was already known to me, though no one then had found it, for it is described in the 'Mahawansa' as being built in a garden by a king who died about the time that Richard Cœur de Lion came to the throne of England. Motors can reach the place now.

Near that ruin with the frescoes I was taught once how acute man's senses might be if he would use them. I was out with a gun and a Veddha boy, when suddenly he halted and said he could smell a leopard. After a while I thought I could smell an animal too; but the boy did far more than that, for he followed the scent with his nose held high for several hundred yards before he proved his claim by picking up the fresh track on a patch of soft soil, and we followed it right up to a room in the building of the frescoes, where it led into a sort of cave made by brick debris. I clambered into the dark chamber through a hole in the roof. The leopard had been there, and had gone, and I found on the floor a coin as old as the building.

The last time I visited that city was about twenty years after the adventures I have set down. Where I had gone slowly, we went in a car now; and we found the railway well advanced, and were told that two motor omnibuses called daily. I talked of the better days of old, and my friend envied me; for in the old days it had been an adventure to walk round these ruins that were now so spick and span, with their neat barbed wire fences to keep cattle from damaging the restorations. Beside a rock temple that used to be one of the loneliest and most solemn of places, thousands of people had written their names with bits of brick, or carved them on the stone; and broad roads ran where I had stolen along the paths made by animals.

The place was spoiled, and I told my friend so as I led him a few hundred yards from his car to look at the oldest inscription in the city. This town was not old for Ceylon. It had flourished in the middle ages of Lanka's history, reached the zenith of its curve in the twelfth century A.D., and been abandoned to the jungle two centuries later; but there was one old inscription in the script of one of the first four centuries of our era, and I wanted to see it again. It was cut into a huge boulder, probably by a hermit who had lived there before the city was built, and the rock it adorned made one side of a small cave on the west of a big pile of similar rocks. There was a larger cave on the east, quite open to see into, but sloping down to the back, where it ended in a hole, about the size of the knee-hole of a writing-table, that went under the rocks. Above these caves were tumbled rocks with further holes and caves, and a few bushes; the whole pile being the size of a big farm-house and its outbuildings.

We pushed through the bushes and found the inscription. Then we looked into the larger cave. The floor was covered with the usual soft dust, part decayed rock particles and part bats' guano, and we saw the tracks of porcupines and of a mongoose, as we would have expected had we given the matter a thought. It was decidedly more curious to see the track of a fair-sized crocodile leading across the cave and down into the knee-hole den that ran beneath the rock. The tank was about a mile away, but there were pools nearer, and crocodiles sometimes travel far on foot.

Stranger by far than the crocodile's track was the trail of a bear, who had walked along the reptile's path and followed him down into the dark den beyond. We could find no other exit, and no tracks led out.

This extraordinary puzzle we failed to solve. The Ceylon bear does not hunt live game, except termites and their larvæ. This bear was full grown, and, of course, an animal with vast experience of jungle life. The strongest sense a bear has is that of smell, and a crocodile smells strong; but apart from that, a bear is no fool, and even a human child could have read the track and known that the crocodile had gone into the den; for that soft dust takes a perfect impression, and the very wrinkles on the saurian's soles were clear enough for a palmist to have told his fortune; and yet we could not do so! It is beyond possibility that the bear went in ignorance that the crocodile had gone before him; but why did he follow? Even in the open a bear would have little chance in a fight with a crocodile of that size, and in a cave none whatever. With us was a Tamil man, an old friend of mine, wise in wood-craft, and he was as mystified as we were. He told us that a cave in the upper storey of the pile was sometimes occupied by a leop-ardess, who had given birth to cubs there a year before; and, as we left by a narrow foot-path that led on to some further ruins, we found ourselves treading in her tracks, for she had visited the pile of rocks that very morning.

This was enough, and I took back all I had said about the place being spoiled; but I do not think the age of petrol can be resisted much longer. It happened in October 1925, and the name of the city is Polonnaruwa.

Thinking it over afterwards, I wondered if the solution might be that a crocodile, who had been wounded, had crawled into the den and died there, and that the bear knew he was dead. But, after all, even we would have known that! So the puzzle remains unsolved.

Above that ruined city lies its tank, one of the loveliest things in the world. The waters are very blue, and in the far distance, across a plain where men are rarer than bears, the peaks and ramparts of the mountain ranges tower into the sky to a height of six thousand feet or more. They too are vivid blue, but a different blue from the water. To walk round the tank may take two hours, or three if it be very full, and even now one is sure to see crocodiles there; but the most delightful part of it is in the forest of red lotuses, so full of birds that their voices mingle in a clatter like that of a children's playground. Once when I shot a crocodile there, a man strode from the grass where he had lain hid while I stalked the sleeping creature to slay it. He was tall, and he was dignified with the dignity that scorns clothes, and as he smote the dead animal with his bare foot, he reviled it in a loud voice, for had it not swallowed his goat, bell and all, bell and all, as he kept repeating.

That city is well known. Guide-books describe it, and there will soon be an hotel there with picture post-cards for sale. But I know another city where no one ever goes, and where no building has yet been dug out so far as I know. Like all the ancient towns of the Sinhalese, it lies below the bund of an enormous tank whose area may well have been thousands of acres, for the bund is miles long. But now the very name of the tank is lost, for the bund burst hundreds of years ago and its bed is but a low-lying region in the unbroken forest, a deeper area amid the sea of trees. The only name it now bears is a Tamil one meaning Tank of the Great Breach.

At a water-hole in a rock in the bed of that tank I saw a bear stoop and drink, and it was curious to think how he sought for that small hole of stagnant water, as for a rare treasure, in a place that for many centuries was at the bottom of an inland sea where waves broke and pelicans sailed in fleets. More than anything else it brought home to me most vividly how brief had been the age of tanks in the long history of the jungle. For a million years animals drank from that narrow hole; then for a thousand years the rock, hole and all, was underneath the waves; and now the jungle drinks again where animals drank when man used stone arrowheads, and before he invented them, and before nature invented him.

When the bund burst, and the tank rushed out to seek the sea, a deep channel was cut through the city. Pottery of varied kinds projects from the banks of the cataclysmic stream, and if I were going to dig into the secrets of that city I should begin there, where a section showing all levels is ready to hand.

For three days I wandered there, and found the pillars and mounds of many buildings, but failed to find what I sought, which was an inscription telling the city's name. The whole of it, and I do not know how wide it may be, is covered in high forest, and the only name it now bears is the name of a tree that abounds there. As a rule, some sort of human occupation persists, but at this place no man lives, and the nearest villagers know nothing whatever of the history of the most truly *buried* city in Ceylon. Yet, if but one word were found, and that the right one, its name, we would probably find that much of its story is already known; for in the 'Mahawansa,' the old chronicle of the Sinhalese, there are many places mentioned that have not yet been identified, and so large a town must surely be one of these.

On the opposite side of the island, on the coast near Mannar, there is another old city of a very different kind. It lies amid sand dunes, where partridge calls are heard, and where few wild animals live but jackals, some deer who manage to extract a livelihood from the scrub, a few monkeys, and the leopards that live on them and the deer. But it is a fine place for birds, and many are common there that are rarely seen in the forests. There are dozens of shrikes; hoopoes are common; I saw a rare and very beautiful woodpecker with a cap of gold on her head there; and in a shallow brackish hollow, where many flamingoes waded, I shot one among a great company of spoonbills, and afterwards ate him and found his flesh good. Flamingo is very eatable too, and so is the great hornbill, whose weird laughter echoes in the forest like the mirth of a goblin. But the bittern is so utterly unfit for human food that even hungry Moormen jib at him. Hunger drives one to try strange foods, and in those Northern jungles a fellow wanderer and I came down to one meal a day of kurakkan and whatever else we could get to flavour it.

When it rained, the dunes might be searched for coins that were left on the surface as the sand washed away, and I picked up many there of divers kinds not altogether expected. For at one time this was the chief port of traffic with India, and it was here that several armies landed that came to harry Lanka.

Coins of various dynasties of South India were found, and of course Roman coins, for they come to light everywhere in Ceylon, and the money of five-and-twenty emperors has been recorded. Roman ships had probably lain in the roadstead off the city of the sand dunes, and Roman sailors may have stared at the ancestors of the monkeys who stared at me as I hunted the sands for finds. The Chinese had been there too, for a coin or two of theirs and a few pieces of their porcelain were left bare by the wind and rain. But perhaps the most unexpected coin of all that are found there is a Sinhalese one, the smallest old Sinhalese coin known, for it is found almost nowhere else at all, even in the capital city of the king who struck it.

While I was camped on the dunes, a fierce storm swept down on us in the middle of the night, and my tent was blown down on top of me. It was a heavy double one, and it broke the rods of my mosquito net and pinned me down beneath its wet folds. I shouted for help, and after some time was glad to hear the feet of running coolies; but alas! they had not come to help me, for their own tent had blown flat too, and they were running to take refuge in mine. So I had to be hospitable, and they crawled in, and we sat in a circle until dawn, with the wet canvas held up on our heads, while the wind roared about the sands and arranged them in new waves that exposed for us to pick up next day more coins, and numbers of pieces of bangles carved from chank shells that once had been worn by the ladies of that ancient city, and perhaps put on to allure Chinese and Roman sailors.

I gained some idea of what that ancient harbour had once looked like when visiting the island of Kayts in the archipelago to the north of Ceylon; for in the roadstead there more than thirty sailing ships were lying. They were of Eastern rig, of Eastern build, and manned and owned by Eastern men; not a single European sailed in any one of them in any capacity. Some had three masts, and some only two, but all were sea-going ships, and between them they visited the coasts of far Arabia and the Persian Gulf, as well as the ports of India and Ceylon. Some, they told me, traded with the remote coral islands in the middle of the Indian Ocean. On the shore two stout ships were being built, and I went aboard one, and was shown round by the designer and head carpenter, a Tamil who knew no English; and as we talked to that well-informed and practical man, it seemed to me that here was a short cut in archæology, and a more direct route to the understanding of the old port buried among the sand dunes than could be found by scouring the sand for coins.

While I searched ruins for coins or bits of pottery, I wondered whether we of the twentieth century may not know more about the history of ancient civilisations than will ever be known again. In Ceylon we do not know much, for the archæology practised there for many years was little more than licensed curio hunting; but in Egypt, Ur of the Chaldees, and elsewhere, very much is known, for they have been scientifically excavated. The question, however, is not what we know now, but what will we know five hundred years hence? Objects found have two quite different kinds of value —æsthetic and evidential. They may have both, or a very little of one and a great deal of the other; but æsthetic value is imperishable and the other is not. A work of art remains equally beautiful if labelled correctly, or if found in a pawnshop described as 'heathen goddess,' but the *whole* value it had as evidence for the historian has gone immediately its precise place of origin is forgotten. A Roman coin found in Rome has almost no value as evidence: found in Ceylon it has more, and if found in the desert in Australia its value would be of quite different degree. When an object is transferred from a ruin to a museum its evidential value no longer consists of its position relative to other objects, but is transferred to certain bits of paper—its label, and the report written about it. Ceylon's ruins yielded many objects whose detailed history was never transferred to paper, so their value as evidence is already lost; but they may not be so very far behind Ur and Hissarlik in another few centuries. A war greater than the last, a period of decay of culture due to some discovery making wealth too easy for our frail natures to stand up to it, or a fungoid disease of paper, any little accident like that might destroy utterly the evidential value of all that has ever been dug from all the buried cities of the earth, and Nineveh and Troy would again be nameless mounds like that city where the bear drinks in the bed of the tank. The people of those cities had knowledge they thought would endure for ever, but how many square yards of their writing mediums in the aggregate now remain? The memories of men are too frail a thread to hang history from. Books are written every year contesting from one side or the other the bare facts of a happening in Palestine that half the world professes to consider the most important thing that ever happened; and that was not even as far back as the inscriptions on the rocks where I followed the stalking buffalo! But far nearer, and in our own country, the history of our greatest poet is so far forgotten that one book has been published to prove he was Bacon, another to prove he was Lord Derby, and others to prove he was himself. Frail is human memory, but is paper less frail? And, save for those two rival frailties, nothing exists to prevent the jungle tide from rising again, and the ruins of London becoming nameless bunkers in golf courses.

But animal life persists, and the trees, and the whole complex interdependent life we call the jungle, be it forest or only sandy dunes, is renewed afresh each time its tide flows, and civilisation sinks. Where the monks who ruled kings built high towers, the wild swine dug for roots before monks were invented, or kings either, and they still dig there. A king of Lanka carved in granite his proud command that the thing he had accomplished should not be set aside "*so long as the sun and the moon endure, and birds build their nests*," and of his memory nothing remains but this scrap of poetry, now grown wistful; for, as he feared might happen to others, so it has happened to him, and his decree has become, in his own words, "*like a line drawn upon water.*"

Looking back to those buried cities for some symbol to crystallise their many-sided appeal, I see the dark bowed figure of that bear as he stooped in the dusk over the one thing the nameless city still could offer—the narrow cleft of water. His lone form, older in shape than ours, rougher, and less complex, gives me my symbol.

THE ANCIENT ROAD

The feet that hollowed the ancient road, by village, or field, or town,
Now trail their way where the moon-beams play, and are loosed when the sun goes down
To haunt the shade of lonely glade, to float by glimmering stream,
Or tread their old-time measures by the fireflies' dancing gleam.

VI. A BORDER LAND

In the north of Ceylon, as of England, there is a border land where two races meet. Very early in the history of the Sinhalese, probably at least as long ago as the fourth century B.C., Tamil princes from the opposite coast of India had seized upon the Jaffna peninsular and the archipelago to the north of Ceylon's mainland, and begun to colonise those coral shores and islands. The capital of the Sinhalese Kingdom, Anuradhapura, grew to power rapidly, and soon established at least a nominal suzerainty over the other principalities of the island; but although its frontiers *de jure* may have been fixed and proclaimed, its frontiers *de facto* varied with the varying abilities of the kings who successively occupied the throne through some twenty centuries of civil and foreign wars. More than one king of Lanka invaded India. Several claimed to have captured the city of Madura, and one at least brought back enough captives to colonise a sparsely populated district of his dominions. Another waged war with a king of Pegu, and intermarriage took place with the royal family of Cambodia, as well as with many royal races of India. At some unknown time the Sinhalese colonised the Maldive Islands, that lone group of coral atols in the middle of the Indian Ocean, and apparently carried Buddhism there. In turn they were themselves invaded countless times by various Indian peoples, several times by Chinese, and at least once by Malays, before the Portuguese began to build forts around their coast.

The northern frontier, where the Tamils and Sinhalese joined hands, ran through a region known as the Wanni, a word close akin to the Sinhalese adjective 'wal,' meaning wild or woodland, and perhaps to the western 'wald,' 'weald,' 'wold,' and possibly 'wild.' And the Wanni is very wild. It is a region where the tide of jungle has flowed so strongly back that the works of men have disappeared beneath a carpet of leaves, like the babes in the wood in the fairy story. It is an old forest, stretching across Ceylon from sea to sea, almost unbroken save by rare hamlets so sunken in its depths that one may walk for days and scarce know of their existence. Along its southern fringe the people are Sinhalese for the most part, though a few Veddhas still linger there whose own language is lost, and who speak Tamil and Sinhalese so impartially that they change from one tongue to the other in the middle of a conversation without effort or any preference either way. North of these, and throughout the whole of the rest of the Wanni, the people are Tamils of various castes who unite but in calling each other Wanniyar.

Two railways and a few roads cut thin lines through the Wanni; but a hundred yards from their hard edges the unaltered jungle has already forgotten the gangs of coolies with axes, and the overseers and engineers with guns, who laboured noisily for a while, killed a few trees and birds and animals, and left in exchange for the stones they blasted from quarries the bones of not few of their fellows who died of malaria, that most real demon of the wilderness. For a few months or years they broke the harmony of centuries, and then went their way, and left the forest once more to that equilibrium of many wars the jungle knows as peace.

Towards the western sea-board the Wanni grows thinner and sparser where its trees fight a losing battle with the sun in the dry coastal belt, until, at last, before the water's edge is reached, the woods have given way to a land of natural links where grass and sand and Palmyra palms seem like a strip of India brought from over the way by the invading Tamils. But on the east coast the forest makes stronger growth, and the trees march down in undepleted regiments to the fences that are built from their branches to keep wild animals out of the cultivated lands of the sea-side villagers. Where villages are lacking, the forest thrusts out still farther, until its outposts carry the battle of sea and land into the lagoons where mangrove trees who refuse to be drowned make haunted tangles of twisted boughs, fit for jabberwocks to roost in, and alive with birds—egrets and herons, bitterns and ducks and divers, pied kingfishers who hover like hawks, and jewelled kingfishers who plunge for crabs they beat to pieces on the snaky boughs. Where neither fields nor lagoons intervene, the forest attains the frontier of the sea itself, and the foremost ranks of the trees stand in the fighting line along spring-tide level, hard and tough and gnarled, until their sloping front of inured twigs, clipped by the sand-blast the sea-gales drive, grows so matted and dense that it looks to be easier to walk up its inclined surface than to push a way through it. But in reality it is tunnelled with many paths, some made by wandering buffaloes, others by deer or wild pigs, and all dotted with the dainty footprints of the leopards whose trail may even be found among the bleached fan-shells, nautilus, cowries, and corals cast by storms above the normal dominion of the sea. In some places quantities of pumice can be found, not of Ceylon origin, for Ceylon has no volcano; and I have wondered if may be it is a last relic of the great eruption when the sea broke into Krakatoa some fifty years ago.

The Wanni knows little of Englishmen, for its thin population demands but little government, and of commerce or industry pursued by white men there is none. Sportsmen come in on raids, stay rarely for so long as a week, kill or wound or miss, and go off again. Men who are not sportsmen sometimes motor along its lonely roads by night, armed with rifle and spotlight, and shoot from their safe cars at dazzled animals staring from the edge of the black forest at the passing devil. No man worth calling such would fire at an animal unless prepared to track it down if wounded, even at some peril of his own skin, and, since night-shooting from a car precludes this act of much mercy and some courage, the cowardly practice should entitle its followers to be expelled from any club used by gentlemen, for some misdemeanours are punished more fitly in this manner than by law.

Twice have I travelled for three months at a time in the Wanni, and met but one white man beside my fellow wanderer; but I heard once of another whose presence there puzzled me sorely. I had walked most of the day since the last village, a hamlet of two huts, and had before me another long march before reaching the next one. The path was a game track, sometimes used by men, and easy for a jungle-dweller to follow though difficult enough for me; and I halted for the night by a water-hole, where I slept beneath the stars on a warm slab-rock. And there I found excellent company, for a party of Veddhas, old friends of mine, were out with their dogs on a hunting trip, and had chosen the same camp for the night: they sat far into the night telling tales of the jungle, tales that is of life as they knew and lived it. They told me then, and I had heard it from them before, that men once wore tails and climbed among the trees as monkeys, and were proud of it in the jesting way that a man might be proud of descending from Robin Hood or Alexander Borgia. Was this merely a legend of the woods, true but by chance, the random flight of fancy of some jungle poet; or was it a lost fragment of knowledge long forgotten? There are so many parallels. When Burton wandered in Somaliland in the eighteen fifties, the natives, he said, did not permit strangers to interfere with the bats that haunted their huts, for these were supposed to live upon mosquitoes, whose bite 'they erroneously believed' to be the cause of fever. Have the Veddhas some ancient memory of a Charles Darwin, and the Somalis of a prehistoric Ronald Ross? Must Wilbur and Orville Wright yield up their laurels to Ravana, King of Lanka in mythical times when the island was inhabited by demons;

for Valmiki the poet, singing some think a thousand years before Christ, describes him as flying from the mountains of South India to the mountains of Lanka in a 'bird machine.' Many have been reputed to fly, but this was a machine, perhaps the same fiery chariot that Elijah used, for these stories travel far, and in the woods of Ceylon many Greek myths may still be found: the very landing of the Sinhalese doubles the story of Ulysses and Circe.

Not long before, these Veddhas said, a white man had travelled along that path alone. They had met him and guided him to the water-hole we sat by, and had shared their food with him, for he had none of his own. He was travelling northward, without gun or guide or baggage, and he could neither speak nor understand Sinhalese or Tamil, a thing which precludes his having been a man of the country as completely as his lack of baggage proves him not to have been either a Government servant or a sportsman. He puzzled those Veddhas, and the next day he went on alone, and they never heard of him again. And he puzzled me too, for I never heard of his arriving at the other end, and could meet with no one who had seen what was as remarkable a sight in that wilderness as a Veddha stalking the King's deer would be in Windsor Park. I can but imagine he may have been some sailor or other absconder from a ship, who had taken train and wandered off into the woods, where he probably perished. If this happened I do not think any remains would ever be found, unless by chance a coin or metal button or knife were come upon; for the forest devours its dead very swiftly. I killed a bear once, and dragged the body out to the middle of a wide expanse of slab-rock, where I skinned it; and twenty-eight days afterwards I passed by the same way, and went to the rock to see how much remained. Nothing remained: not one single bone of that stout animal's skeleton. I searched every likely nook, but found not a sign to show a bear had ever died. After the leopards, and perhaps even his brother bears had eaten of him, the lesser creatures had their turn—jackals, cats, and birds, and porcupines who gnaw bones—and the crumbs from their table were swept up by the silent industrious ants who daily scour every inch of the forest floor and polish it up like vacuum cleaners. I once surprised a tiger-cat inside the frame of a dead pig. It was dusk and I saw the pig lying in long grass, and stalked him successfully. With careful aim I shot him, and he lay still; but when I approached, this unexpected animal, who had lain immovable while my bullet passed an inch from him through the pig, sprang forth and raced for covert, and got away before I recovered my wits. A friend of mine shot an elephant near a tank, and went weeks later to see what remained of his giant carcass, and when he drew near it, out there poured a covey of crocodiles who had burrowed right into the dreadful corpse and were eating it up from inside. Something like this would happen to a man, and termites would devour his clothes and boots equally rapidly. For the jungle dissolves and recreates over and over and over again, as the Hindu philosophers perceived millenniums ago and built their religion on it. All that we know of things that died more anciently than a month ago is written in stone or brick or earthwork, or, perhaps more durable even than these, in legend.

Some of the oldest of all written records in Ceylon were found in the Wanni on a long low hill, a petrified whale half submerged in the sea of trees, where so many inscriptions of the earliest Buddhist times are carved in the rocks that it took me four days' hard work to copy those I found, and probably there are as many more I missed. For the place is a labyrinth of clefts and caves and boulders, all overgrown with forest wherever the trees can find earth enough to lodge their roots, and tangled up with octopus-like fig-trees, and creepers, and thorny cuphorbias, where no earth at all appears to surround the roots that dig into sun-scorched cracks among the rocks. The hill is less than a mile long, and not more, I think, than two hundred feet high; but at one time it must have been the abiding place of hundreds of monks, for every possible sheltered corner shows some sign of their sojourn there. In some places steps are sunk into the rocks; in others, deep rock-cut grooves show where walls were founded, or square socket-holes remain that once held the bases of wooden pillars. Some of the rock surfaces besides the water-holes are pitted with circular holes, whose worn sides suggest they may have been mortars to pound grain in; but the caves beneath the boulders give the plainest picture of what must have been one of the earliest monasteries in Southern Asia, as old to St Thomas, if his travels took him there, as St Paul's is to Londoners to-day. The boulders have natural hollows beneath them, or sometimes only overhanging sides, where with little art shallow depressions were scooped or worn in the hard stone floors and used by ascetics for their beds. The open caves thus formed were closed by brick walls, and above these, where they joined the rock above, drip-ledges were cut so that rain-water should pass away outside the cave. In the rock brows above the drip-ledges the inscriptions were cut in that old alphabet which fathered every script of India and further India, except those derived from the Arabic writing brought in many centuries later. Tamil, Sinhalese, Burmese, Siamese, Tibetan, one of the alphabets of Japan, another of Java, and a score of Indian alphabets find common origin in the characters cut in these rocks, and used in several of his inscriptions by Asoka, the first great Emperor of India to adopt Buddhism as his faith. None of the inscriptions give the old name of the monastery, though they preserve the names of several kings and princes that enable them to be dated back to the middle of the third century B.C., when Tissa Beloved by the Gods received from Asoka the message of The Wise One, Siddhattha Buddha. Sinhalese tradition says that Asoka's own son was the missionary. Most of the uppermost caves are situated beneath enormous boulders which lie upon the bare back of the hill, above the tangle of the jungle, scattered in a row as though left there by giants at play. In front of their doors the space is narrow before a precipice falls to the woods below, for the eastern side is well-nigh unscaleable. The site is charming, and the monks could look out over a marvellous view, now many tinted with the varied colours of the tops of forest trees, then probably fields and gardens: on clear days they must have seen the sea. It was a delightful place to live, but what allured me mostly was the precipice; for it must have happened often that small objects rolled over the cliff's edge and were lost, and the monks probably found the abyss a convenient dumping-place for the sweepings of their cells, broken dishes and bowls, beads from broken rosaries, and the like. The rubbish of one age makes the treasures of another. The contents of the servants' hall of the seventeenth century sell as valuable antiques in the twentieth; and the rubbish of those monks of ancient time would be eagerly sought by museums now. When I was there I had no time to pursue this thought, for it would have entailed felling trees and much earth-cutting; but it seems worth following up by some more leisurely explorer.

The border line between Sinhalese and Tamil, where they met and traded or fought, shifted north or south as the power of the overlord at Anuradhapura waxed or waned, and in the days of the monastery was farther north than now; for the neighbouring villagers are Tamils and Hindus, to whom the hill is not sacred, and its ruins of no interest whatsoever. The old name is lost, and the names the hills bear now, for there are two crests, are Tamil, and mean respectively Hill-of-Bats and Big-Tamarind-Tank-Hill. None of the inscriptions I found were later in date than four or five centuries after the monastery's foundation, so it seems likely that the hill was early abandoned to the bears who inhabit it now. It interested me to find the requirements of monks and bears so nearly identical; and just as the earliest monks showed a preference for converting the dens of bears into hermits' cells, so do bears to-day prefer the sites of ruined monasteries, thus offering a very sincere tribute in retrospect to men who had professed to exchange the temptations of an over-luxurious world for a life of bodily simplicity and rigorous contemplation. When I lived in Anuradhapura in 1902, the priest of Issurumuniya temple there delighted to tell how, thirty years earlier, he had found the little cave temple inhabited by a she-bear, whom the villagers evicted so that he might live there in her place.

In one cave at the top of the Hill-of-Bats I found the mummified corpse of a crocodile, whose skin had proved too hard or unpalatable even for the porcupines' chisel teeth. Its presence there was but one more illustration of the distance crocodiles will travel. I have sometimes wondered if these journeys are undertaken to secure a peaceful end, safe from the jaws of their cannibal companions; but who knows? It may be that one in a thousand travels to see the world. Where this corpse had desiccated there were no termites, for there was no vegetation; but I am surprised that the hornets had not found the feast, for they are indefatigable removers of nuisances. I watched once through field-glasses a swarm of hornets carrying off little piecemeal the body of a dead crocodile that I could smell too strongly quite two hundred yards away.

In all the border land the Hill of the Tamarind is the best example of the earliest form of rock monastery where natural features were preserved almost unchanged, and where the illusion was fostered of living on a mountain. This was a dream very precious to early Buddhists, relaying, perhaps, an echo of the divine myths that hang like clouds around the Himalayas as around Olympus · for when the monasteries became enormous establishments, wealthy, and proud, and powerful enough to guide the destinies of kings, they still employed in ornament on the facades of the temples and monastic palaces conventional patterns that signify mountains, and caves, and the rustic dens of bears. Yet they had real mountains to live in not so very far away, and had only to walk up-stream along their own irrigation channels and the contributing brooks to come to them had they wished to; but they preferred the plains, and every little outcrop of rock in the Wanni has done service as a miniature mountain, bears the traces of monastic occupation a thousand or two thousand years ago, and the footprints and droppings of bears of to-day. Where there are caves there are inscriptions, still clear to read two thousand years after their chisellers have gone. Not much is to be learned from them as a rule, though their style gives their date in round centuries. Nearly always they are simple records of grants and gifts made to the Order, with the names of the donors, and a formula of welcome to the monks of the four quarters of the Buddhist world "both present and absent"—that is to say, living and to come. In most lands archæology deals with temples whose last worshipper died long centuries ago. No one now prays to Horus or to Pallas Athene (not under that name); but here in the forests of Ceylon the ruins we explore are those of a religion still living, to this day the faith of the majority of the population. It would seem, therefore, that these deeds of gift, carved in stone and sometimes bearing the names of kings, might be held in equity to entitle the church to resume its property at will. But it is not so in law, and, all things considered, perhaps this is as well, though it is more debateable than most officials would concede.

It was while hunting for inscriptions in the Wanni that I saw a real miracle performed in broad daylight. A hunter had promised to show me an inscribed pillar that lay on the ground six or seven miles away in uninhabited jungle, and I had walked there, taking with me several coolies to carry tools and food, and to turn over the pillar. The man was as good as his word, and led me to a royal grant of about the ninth century A.D. Where there had been a monastery a thousand years before all was now thorny tangle, and a herd of wild elephants surrounded us and disturbed me while I was taking particulars and trying to decipher the titles of the king. It occupied me some time, and the sun was near the tree-tops when I was ready to start for camp. There was no water very near, and neither the hunter nor I wished to pass the night among the elephants; so we moved off, and then one of the coolies trod upon a very large centipede and was bitten in the soft part of the foot below the inside ankle-bone. The poor fellow suffered great agony, and not only was unable to bear his foot upon the ground, but complained of violent pain in the groin. We had enough to do to get back to camp before dark without having a man to carry, and I was beginning to resign myself to the company of the elephants, and was mournfully shaking my water-bottle when the miracle began to take place. It was the hunter who performed it, as was only fair, for he knew the local gods better than we did. He caused the bitten man to sit upon the grass with his legs extended, and squatted opposite to him on his heels. From his pocket he drew the usual outfit of a chewer of betel, and took lime on the end of his finger and drew with it a chalky line around the patient's ankle. Then he placed the tips of the fingers of his two hands upon the patient's thigh, high up and touching the painful groin, and drew them down slowly toward the foot, while he called in a loud voice by name upon several *munis* or spirits, his words being strung together in a versified charm or incantation. As his fingers passed the chalk line he gave a shout that apparently completed the eviction of the poison, for the wounded man rose, took up his burden, and walked. As to how it was done there were only two opinions, and probably both were wrong. I called it suggestion in my mind, and the rest attributed it unhesitatingly to the power of the charm. But what suggestion may be, or what is charm, or what is the physiological action of either I do not pretend to know. I strongly suspect that both words, 'suggestion' and 'charm' (Tamil *mantaram*), alike only serve, like so many words we use, to veil our unbroken ignorance of the mechanism of the miracle. Reward was neither offered nor demanded, and both men were only anxious that the discomfort of a night in the woods should be avoided by any fair means. No question of malingering arose, and the whole thing passed with slight comment, though, of course, it was recited with other adventures of the day while we sat round our comforting camp fire in the evening.

It is so much easier to say how mysterious things do *not* happen than how they *do*; and all the guesses, demonological, magical, and otherwise, lead as often as not through kaleidoscopic changes of words into the shrines of emptiness, not rendered sacred by ideas.

In the Wanni a new cult is in the making, a branch religion, or perhaps only a bud as yet, growing on the hoary old trunk of wood-god worship. Somewhat less than a hundred years ago an Englishman ruled the north as a raja in the way that men could rule before telegraphs and railways caused self-reliance to atrophy, and scaled down administrators to the level of postmen's slaves. Already his name is legend, and soon his personality will be merged into one of the local gods, as was the personality of Mahasena, who built Minneriya tank some fifteen centuries ago. In one way, indeed, this great man already pervades the Wanni, for men say that he fathered a child in every village within its borders, but perhaps this is only a form of flattery. A story of his unbending pride was told me as having indubitably happened in several distinct and widely separated places. He rode along a forest path upon a white horse, and met an elephant in the narrow way. He shouted, and the elephant trumpeted, but neither would give way and allow the other to pass, until the hero struck spurs into his horse, and made him spring over the elephant's head, for the man could not brook that he should turn aside, even for the king of the jungle.

One may see from this that strange things happen in the Wanni, and here is another, better attested. It is one of the driest regions in Ceylon, and yet holds one of the greatest world's records for rainfall, carefully measured at the time by an irrigation engineer. Thirty-two inches fell in twenty-four hours, as much as falls in London in one year and four months; yet London seems a wet place, and the Wanni a very dry one. I was there once for three months and saw but one shower. It caught two of us far from camp at sunset, just when we were settling down for a snug night in the open without a tent. A chill meant fever, and we could hear the storm roaring like a shingle beach as it rushed across the tree-tops towards us. There was nowhere to go, so we did the next best thing: we tore off our clothes, rolled them into bundles, and curled our bodies round them as a cat curls round her kittens. When the rain had done sluicing off our naked and waterproof backs we had dry clothes to get into.

We went very hungry that trip, as men mostly do who set out to live on the country without supplies; and before we came out to the lagoons and fattened up on fish we grew lean and hard on a diet of smoke-dried wild buffalo. I had to shoot one lest my pack bull Bashan should come to be sacrificed. The buffalo had swum out into a tank, and I had to wade nearly breast-deep to come within range. The very night before we had been disturbed by loud spanking sounds, much as though an oar were smitten broad-bladed upon water, and creeping along through the sedges that skirted the tank we had been witnesses of a strange moonlight battle between several crocodiles who were quarrelling over the corpse of a cow they had killed. For some reason they had not dragged it into deep water, but were devouring it on the grass, swinging at each other with their great flat tails, and making the curious spanking noise we had heard in our tent. However, we were exceedingly hungry, and I went on after the buffalo. I fired two shots, and he galloped through the shallows and disappeared into the thorny jungle that grew right down to the water's edge at the back of the tank. I followed more slowly, and then for three and a half hours followed his blood-trail through dense thorn and scrub, sometimes stooping, sometimes on hands and knees, and always in fear lest his mud-stained horns and pain-maddened eyes should burst through the thorns and charge home before I had time to aim.

For buffaloes have an instinctive habit of circling on their tracks to hunt their hunter. And in the end this happened, though not as I had pictured it among the thorns; for before he turned we had worked through into high forest without undergrowth, and in the evening light, in those dim aisles of the woods, he came charging gallantly, lance in rest, and died bravely, as he deserved to do. Some forms of slaying seem to me scarcely more chivalrous than laying down poison, but the death of that buffalo lies less heavily on my conscience than any other death I have caused, for he made me know fear more closely than any other opponent ever did. For several weeks we lived on his dried meat in some discomfort; but not equal to that which arose from the discovery of a rich orchard of wild wood-apples where elephants had been feeding greedily, for we found them so palatable that we laid in a stock of fruit and ate puddings made from it every day for a week, thereby confirming a medical discovery the observant jungle people had made perhaps before their tails fell off, but had omitted to tell us of, that wood-apple pulp is an admirable substitute for chlorodine.

The human population of the Wanni is small, but of monkeys there is no end. Everywhere among the tree-tops their roads run, with well-tried bridges where branches meet high above crocodile-haunted pools; and across the rocks, too, they have well-worn routes and passes, where each projecting handhold has grown smooth and polished by the contact of countless small hard palms through the ages. I have even climbed by these prehistoric paths, but they are too difficult to follow far.

Sometimes even monkeys themselves find their aerial ways deceitful, or perhaps it may be that they try new paths too speedily and so come to grief, for twice I have found them fallen. Both were alive, and I killed both, for I could not bear that that last service should be left to the fighting ants. It was in the woods of the old Tamarind monastery that I found the first. He lay upon the floor of the forest with closed eyes, breathing stertorously, for he suffered, I think, from concussion of the brain. In one hand he still grasped tightly a leafy twig of the tree above him, evidence of the nature of his fall. I was alone, and he never knew he died. It was in the western Wanni that I found the other, in the bed of a dry stream where I noticed a peculiar mark as though a sack had been trailed along the sand, followed it up, and came upon a monkey with a broken back dragging himself along by his hands. Poor animal, the red ants were already on his track—remorseless, relentless, tireless, and innumerable,—and I raised my gun to give him the only peace his world had left, the boon I should myself have prayed for. But before the monkey died a strange thing happened. I had invited to come with me a young Christian Tamil clerk, a timid little townsman who would scarce have ventured to walk into even the fringe of the jungle alone; and suddenly this uninspiring man showed heroic quality, for he forbade me to kill the monkey. Let it live its little life! he pleaded, and more than pleaded. I lowered my gun, and talked quietly with him about the misery of the monkey's end: I showed him the column of pursuing ants, spoke of the hours of such pain that a leopard would come as a kind angel, described the monkey with his eyes eaten out, unspeakable horrors. But the little timid man, in his ignorance of nature's calm indifference to what we term justice, still hoped that a miracle would happen and the jungle show kindness to one of its failures. "It has so little: do not take that!" he said; and I thought he might strike me when I fired, but he only wept. Nevertheless my respect for him was immense, and I wish it seemed possible he could have grown to realise I was not the demon of cruelty he believed. But in such matters as these the views of righteousness held by East and West sometimes diverge so widely that one can only try to respect the ideals of other men without sharing or even comprehending them. In a village in the Wanni I was shown a crocodile who had not fed for six months, but the villagers did not wish me to destroy him, though they hunted deer for food, and were not averse from showing game to sportsmen. In a thicket by the village an abandoned well had caved in and become a barrel-shaped hole with a collar of roots projecting inwards and making of it a perfectly effective trap. Two animals had fallen in, a crocodile five or six feet in length, and a truly gigantic mud-turtle who must have proved too hard a nut to crack, for the villagers had known both animals for six months when I saw them alive. In rainy weather a few frogs may have leaped in, but nothing else.

When at last we came through the forest and approached the sea, we saw the lagoons from the top of a little hill, half a day's march away. The curious beauty of their pale colours and luminous purity were so amazingly alluring to the eyes after some months in forest that I thought the picture more like some dainty artist's vision of fairyland than a piece of real earth and water. When we camped next day beside Kokkilay and bathed in its waters, warm as tea and free from crocodiles or sharks, I knew that a more perfect place to linger for a few months aloof from the modern world could scarce be found. Many of the wading birds that ran along the shore were new to me, and scores of larks sang in the air, soaring as our English skylarks do, though not to so great a height. On the sea side of the lagoon, in the narrow tongue of land separating its salt waters from the salt waves of the Indian Ocean, fair fresh water, good enough to drink, could be had for the trouble of scooping a hole two or three feet deep in the soft sand above high-water mark. It made me wonder whether the early explorers of Australia —Gray, Eyre, and the rest who suffered so dreadfully from thirst—may conceivably have had potable water close to hand in an unthought-of situation. But of all the joys of that delightful camp, to us and to our coolies the fish came first, for we were really on the edge of starving, and I had gone barefoot for three weeks because my feet would no longer fit into my boots, an indirect result of malnutrition. We rested, bathed, watched birds, and ate fish for several days, and then pursued our hunt for inscriptions, which was the ruling motive for the journey.

Kokkilay covers many square miles, but the flamingoes can wade all over it, and they go so far out that they are seen only as pale-pink spots on the pale-blue inland sea. There is a mystery about the flamingoes of Ceylon. At one time I collected records of their presence, and found that flocks had been observed, and not rarely, in every month of the year. This would seem to preclude their being migrants, and yet they are not known to nest in Ceylon. Since they are remarkably noticeable birds and nest in large colonies, this seems to be a little problem some local ornithologist might like to look into.

On the spit of land between lagoon and sea I found the fossils of sea-shells, evidence of upheaval; and within a few hundred yards of this there lay the débris of a village washed now by the high tides, showing subsidence, so the levels have oscillated. But of late they appear to have been stable, for on the end of a promontory running out into the lagoon there is a little stone Hindu temple some five or six centuries old, now in ruins, though enough remains to show what a perfect little gem of its rather florid style it must have been. The villagers have a legend that their lagoon was once a mighty stretch of paddy-fields, and the legend may be true, and green waves of bright young rice have rippled in the sea breeze that now ripples the blue lagoon; for one of the very largest of the ancient Sinhalese storage tanks, built a thousand years before the temple on the promontory, is hidden in the forest not too far away. It is now a swamp in wet weather, and a prairie in dry, a great open island of grass in the sea of forest, and a notable haunt of wild buffaloes; but in its prime there must have been thousands of acres of fields below it, and probably a town; and even now its channel seems to lead to Kokkilay lagoon.

So the tide of the jungle and the tide of

the sea have combined to cover Lanka's border land where, for the while at any rate, man is among the least of the animals.

At earlier causes of abandonment we can guess, if indeed abandonment is the right word to describe a process of withdrawal wherein towns shrank to villages and villages to little hamlets, and then to nothing but mounded cities of the termites. But of one cause that operated in our own time evidence still remains. No longer do princes bring Tamil armies across the straits to raid the temples of Lanka, but quite recently, within the memory of men still living, the stream of Tamil labourers that flowed from India to work on the coffee estates in the mountains used to pass through the south of the Wanni, and they left their mark there. The coolie ports were on the west coast, and men, women and children marched in by two main routes to join the north road that runs as a backbone the length of the plain. Resting sheds and wells remain as monuments of this influx along the northernmost of these two routes, that through the Wanni itself; but the southern route is utterly abandoned, and runs through a stretch of three hundred thousand acres of jungle in which no man lives. South of it there is a game sanctuary, and the road itself is rapidly disappearing between the ranks of the invading trees. Under tea in Ceylon there are some four hundred and twenty-five thousand acres, so this uninhabited region may be measured by comparison with that. When the game sanctuary came to be settled under the waste lands ordinance, I assisted to inspect it, and it fell to my duty to examine an old register of land taxes written in Sinhalese and kept in a Government office, and in this I found that as lately as the eighteen sixties fields were still cultivated in what is now the heart of the sanctuary. The explanation was that the immigrants had left cholera in their wake, and this had proved the final straw in man's conflict with the wilderness.

That abandoned road is haunted now, and when I camped there and left my cart in the middle of its grassy track, a man who slept on the straw in the cart woke with a yell that roused the camp, and was found sitting on the hard earth. I lit a lamp and looked into things, for he said he had been pulled out by a leopard; but there was no wound, and the grave old tracker laughed. "It is the gods," he said, "who walk the road by night, and if the cart be dragged out of their fairway the man may sleep on the straw in peace." So we dragged the cart into the edge of the wood, and, as the tracker predicted, they all slept in peace. But not I, for I lay awake listening to the voices of the woods, and cherishing that picture of the gods striding along the forsaken road, and interfering with the sons of men as they did in Hellas three thousand years before.

Very many years after that adventure I was a member of a Commission that inquired into the causes of a railway accident in the Wanni. One difficulty, it appeared, arose from the reluctance of men to patrol the line by night, and it was assumed that this was due to their fear of wild animals. But a member of the Commission, an elderly Tamil gentleman of far higher scholastic attainments than most of us, and one who had held high office under the Crown, explained that this was not so. The greater danger came from the devils who, it was notorious, abounded in the Wanni. I thought of the forsaken road, and supported his argument before a sceptical meeting blinded by new wisdom; and afterwards I obtained from him much wise and valuable direction regarding the best ways to combat devils. I have not forgotten his words, and should classical Christian exoteric theology prove some day to be correct, I may still have hopes of a career, not without brilliance, in another sphere.

Where a population subject to caste rules becomes very thin there is a noticeable loss of vigour, whether cause or effect it is difficult to say; but there are certain factors it may be interesting to consider. It becomes difficult to avoid the interbreeding of cousins more or less close in degree. In the tropics a maiden is not left long unmarried after she is old enough, and the would-be bridegroon is limited by this factor in advance, for where the period of suitability is short the number of girls available is much reduced. He is limited again by lack of transport, for his parents who arrange the marriage only know people within walking distance, and these will be few. Another limitation is a system of reckoning relationship so that cousins who are the children respectively of a brother and sister are eligible to marry, whereas cousins whose mothers are sisters or whose fathers are brothers are within the degree of prohibition. But most sternly is he limited by caste, for of a dozen villages within the range of his travel, perhaps three-quarters or more are inhabited by folk of other caste than his, with whose daughters marriage is unthinkable. All these limiting factors are operating in the Wanni; and while I was there I could not help wondering if one of the invigorating effects of Mahomedan conquest in parts of India may not have come from its effective elimination of caste, the strongest limiting factor of all. Conversion would soon bring about cross-fertilisation of the race, and quite possibly would revive it in a way that Christianity is powerless to do; for though Christian converts learn to eat together, with difficulty, their caste feeling is hardly ever so totally suppressed as to permit freely approved intermarriage as in Mahomedan society.

But no such destiny of religious change is coming in the Wanni. Its jungles are rich in ruins of shrines once holy, both Buddhist and Hindu, but curiously enough its most holy place where active worship still persists belongs to neither of these creeds, though it is approached by the followers of both. The old temples are forgotten, and Islam has never had a foothold there. The wood-god cult is wholly unorganised, and remains a matter of private and personal converse with God. But in the very middle of the forest, hidden farther from cities than any other church in Ceylon, there is an old Roman Catholic mission, so catholic indeed that men and women of all creeds flock there on pilgrimage, and I have even known a strict Mahomedan to go there from Anuradhapura, carrying with him his sick baby son in full faith that he would be healed there. As on the summit of Adam's Peak, where all religions meet without rancour, so at Madu in the Wanni do men and women of many creeds find some common denominator which reduces their divergent faiths to hopes possessed by all; and in the wilderness of this old border land of many wars they find a place of truce.

A PASS THROUGH TIME

THE little hush that followed seemed to him
An immeasurable interlude between two times,
Before, and after: and the shades so dim
Seemed aisles of a mighty temple, whose belfry chimes
Were songs of frogs, and the rush of the hidden stream,
And minivets scattering silver through the air.
The smiling wood-god stirred as he dreamed his dream,
And a shaft of loving sunlight toyed with her hair.

On through unfathomable space the earth still spun,
But the two great halves of time were as cliffs held wide
Till the narrow abiding place he had dared, and won,
Shrank, and the cliffs closed in on either side.

VII. A GIANT HELD CAPTIVE

A GOOD many years ago, in the height of the sou'-west monsoon, when the hot wind had sucked up the waters of the northern plain until tanks and rivers ran dry and the animals were obliged to concentrate near water-holes, I camped beneath a majestic tree on the bund of a village tank. A score of the lean brown people of the hamlet came to renew friendship and see the sights. Their homes were a cluster of mud huts below the tank, whose water ran past their doors into fields that spread for half a mile below. These, and a few patches of dry cultivation hidden in the forest, were all they had to live on, and each separate piece of cultivated land was fenced round by a barricade of branches reinforced by stakes and interwoven until it resisted the invasions of deer and pig and buffalo, and would keep out all but the most determined wild elephants. As for the birds, colonies of weaver birds, flocks of little munias, and of screaming long-tailed parroquets, they were entitled to what they could get, and powder was too costly to be wasted on them. Other enemies were malevolent godlings, or devils, especially one named Kadawariya, who took mighty toll of the crops, and had under his command countless hosts of caterpillars and other pests and blights. East and west of this village forest spread to the sea, almost unbroken save by rare villages with their fields and tanks; and north and south it spread from the foot of the central mountains to the outskirts of industrious Jaffna, where swarms of human beings hide their activity behind fences of palm leaves. Where the forest covers the earth there was once a populous kingdom, to which Jaffna was tributary, and the woods are full of its ruins; but now it has gone back to the jungle again, and the scars men made are healed.

The realm of the great Buddhist kings belongs now to the beasts, and to the gods above them, under whose rule it is apportioned out as though among different tribes; and indeed it is possible that tribal boundaries may have been the origin of the territorial divisions now at last losing their sharp edges under the power of attrition of motor-omnibuses. The wood gods are one of the many unexplored features of the old religion, which lies imbedded in the lower strata of the Buddhism that went over it as a tidal wave in the third century before Christ. Some of the evidence is now fossilised, but much still lives, and among the more vital is the belief in wood gods. In the hills around Adam's Peak the local god takes the name of Saman. Farther north, in the Matale hills and for a long way down into the plain, it is Minneri-deyyo ; and where I was camped it was my old protector Ayanar. I had been counted among his followers for some years ; for those who would know the forests must not stop at the ways of beasts and the dialects of men, but must extend their study in all seriousness to the higher sphere of superhuman powers, or they will not be told the secrets they wish to learn. It is not difficult, for it can never be hard to let people persuade themselves that you have the common-sense to share their belief in things that among them seem obvious to the meanest intelligence ; and it seems wise to get close to the thoughts of people one is thrown among so intimately as when camped together ; but there are some whose racial aloofness forbids it, and who believe the best way of maintaining their own position is to segregate their minds inside a barrier impassable to knowledge. In any case, to know these jungle people it is essential first to comprehend that the gods who walk the woodland ways, the devils who blast crops, the unknown *Thing* that beats a drum at night on the top of an unscaleable rock, and the ghosts who have neither form nor voice nor substance, but only smell, are as truly existent to the villagers as the elephants who trample their kurakkan crop or the leopards who slay their cattle. It is not easy to find any order among the drifting forms of ghosts, and perhaps no one will ever systematise these intertangled vague beliefs; but what matter, the people themselves do not understand it, and do not expect you to; so it is simple as well as polite and wise to conform to jungle ways while in the jungle. The old tracker places his tiny offering upon two leaves fixed on forked twigs thrust into the ground, and uplifts his voice in earnest and dignified prayer to a god who has neither shrine nor image, but whose presence pervades the woods of his kingdom; a god who is friendly to man for the most part, and whose powers are great though by no means unlimited. Like others of his kind, Ayanar is a jealous god, and has been known to smite with blindness those who neglect the simple courtesy of hanging a leafy twig across a bough when entering his domain. It sets the tracker at peace with the unseen world to conform with this custom, and ranks those who do so among the well-informed.

Once upon a time I lay upon a camp-bed beneath an awning slung from two trees on a day so hot that I wore only the legs of my pyjamas. A few trees away five or six jungle men chatted in low voices, taking care not to disturb me or intrude on my privacy. We were hidden as completely as though we were in a room, for all around the little circle we had cleared parched shrubs hedged us in, their leaves gone apricot colour in the heat. Suddenly a roar like the bark of a great dog startled the camp; and by the time I had sprung back from my dreams into life, a she-bear burst through the wall of tinted leaves and charged the camp. I leaped to a rifle, and killed her at my feet; and when I looked round, Kapurala stood behind me holding my shot-gun as though he were a keeper and I shooting driven partridges. He told me afterwards that no one was really afraid, because my rifle had been placed all the previous night before a hollow tree, where it became *blessed* by Ayanar; and I, of a race whose ancestors kept vigil over their arms, and whose regiment's colours have undergone much the same treatment, cannot see that he was either more or less sublime or ridiculous than a bishop.

These people knew me well, and in the outskirts of my camp the children stood and stared, naked or nearly so, brown and rather solemn, with stomachs distended not with food, but by the malaria that enlarges their spleens and shortens their lives. Before the tent four or five grown and bearded men squatted and debated plans of campaign.

I was young in those days, and bloodthirsty I fear, or at any rate full of ardour for the chase. Afterwards I took to better things, and with the same trackers used to go out to see but not to kill, and found it far more interesting, quite as dangerous, and productive of a feeling of virtue that cannot have been wholly due to self-esteem. But at the time I was out to kill as many as I could of certain unfortunate forms of life's loveliness that have been cursed with the title of 'game,' or, more luckless still, of 'vermin.' Crocodiles came under the latter heading, and from man's standpoint naturally so, for where they abound he does not use their leather, and to him they are utterly useless. Also they eat his dogs and his goats, and drag his cattle into muddy water, with soft noses clamped in man-trap jaws, while the poor beast drives his sliding hoofs into the unhelpful mud, and pulls against the pain until he is drawn under and drowned. Even now I can feel small pity for the hundred or more crocodiles I have killed. I had shot some that morning, and now the wise men of the jungle were debating what we should do next. Finally, it was decided to make for the bed of a river some ten miles away, and next morning we went there.

We found our river had ceased to run. Here and there pools of water, bitter with the roots of trees, still lay in the deeper shadier reaches; but for the rest it had become a ribbon of sand, and a highway for thirsty beasts. For though there was no water on the surface it lay not far beneath, and when we, like the other animals, had dug our hole, water soon trickled into it and we were able to fill a kettle. Here I first saw used the bean whose function is to render muddy water clear. Kapurala rubbed the inside of an earthen pot with one, and poured in muddy water, and in a few minutes it settled, the sediment was precipitated, and we were able to decant off clear water fit to drink. To men of the jungle the whole forest is a free store of nearly all they may require; the bark of one tree makes string, that of another is pungent and good to chew when tobacco is scarce, and of a third, infused in boiling water, provides a safe and powerful purgative; one leaf is cool and healing when bound upon ulcers, another yields emollient juice that relieves the itch of tick bites, a third if applied in a compress is said to make dislocations easy to reduce, and a fourth holds some occult value in the practice of the submerged religion of the people. Kapurala used to say that no tree grew which had not some value to man; but as he was guide, hunter, doctor, priest, and story-teller in chief his definition of value was a wide one. Twice he was with me when dangerous beasts charged home, and he never flinched; but there grows to be less scope for such men as the jungle tide ebbs once more, and officials multiply and spawn regulations, for the love of individual freedom that makes a fine tracker leads them into trouble with the law, and litigation goes far to ruin them body and soul.

The stream we camped in had cut deep into the earth, and now that its bed was dry, it had become a sunken road marched upon by many animals. The sides were more than perpendicular, for trees grew up to the very edge, and their exposed and matted roots projected as a fringe from the bank, and made difficult the egress of any who walked the sands except where game tracks, regular animal roads, cut through the banks, and gave access to the forest as lanes that are tributary to a highway.

It was astounding to study the multitude of tracks. Every kind of wild animal had used the road, and many had dug for water as we had. On the sand, footprints were as thickly planted as upon a muddy farm road in England; but instead of horses and sheep and cattle it was elephants and buffaloes, bears and leopards, deer of several kinds, pigs, porcupines, jackals, monkeys, wild cats, and snakes, whose stories were published by the sand. Some of the larger animals, notably bears and elephants, had dug water-holes for themselves, but for the most part the rest had been content to drink at the wells of others. It seemed that we had little need to go farther than this highway of the wild, and we determined to stay where we were.

Tracks are fascinating documents, whether they be the tiny hoof-marks of the mouse deer, whose Sinhalese name, Mi-minna, has been latinised as *memina*, and whose steps show like holes prodded by a pencil, or the huge hip-baths elephants leave in mud, four and a half feet in circumference and nearly two feet deep. They are an endless film of their owner's movements, unrolled as he walks, or trots, or runs, or springs, or lies at rest, and in their unfailing record a first-rate jungle man can read of the animal's hopes and fears, his hunger and his thirst, his love and his war; for all is written on a scroll of life that none can forge. Moreover, it is so intimately attached to its writer that with skill one may estimate his speed and the time gone since he passed, and so compute and plot ahead to prophesy where he is likely to be found, and even what he is likely to be doing. Kapurala and I once spent three days and nights on the track of a wild buffalo bull, eating food we carried with us and drinking where he had drunk. We only saw him once, but at the end I felt we knew him so well that my disappointment at failing to become possessed of his horns was outweighed by a feeling of joy at the escape of a friend from peril.

Early next morning Kapurala went off on some concern of his own, and was away until evening.

I wandered up the stream-bed, and studied

the tracks. The pretty patterns of leopards ran everywhere, but they always exaggerate the news, for leopards are restless wanderers who reel out many miles of record every day. Bears had gone by in ones and twos, their hind feet leaving curiously human indentations deep in moist sand by the drinking places, wider across the toes and sharper of heel, but yet so like the feet of men that it may have been bears who gave rise to legends of troglodytes and gnomes. I made myself snug among bushes on the bank a couple of miles from camp, and sat there listening, watching, and wondering.

Before my bower tall trees touched hands across the stream, and were the home of a tribe of monkeys whose members were working the branches over for fruit, covering perhaps half an acre as they moved in open order. I watched their homely ways where they sat on boughs and reached for seed-pods and stuffed their mouths even fuller than boys do. Sometimes they scolded their children, or bickered among themselves; but for the most part they lived amicably, and it seemed that the qualities that go to make a good monkey are not different from those that make a good man. To watch the mothers carrying their babies slung below their bodies while they climb, or to see two or three kind friends cleaning each other and catching each other's fleas, is always a delight.

So far these were the only wild animals I

had seen, but soon the jungle telegraph brought news of others. The message was plain and urgent, and it was signalled forward mile by mile as silent-footed fear stole through the wood. Far away, beyond the bend of the stream, I heard the blurt of a sambhur's challenge, and could picture the great woodland stag with head upraised, with nostrils wide and moving, while his trumpet ears moved back and fore questioning vibrations of the air more delicate than those we are able to perceive as sound. I made in my mind a picture of that sentry all alert, but could not tell whether he were stamping in challenge of an equal, or whether his hoofs were dug into the soil in readiness for a spring towards safety, or whether he only belled in vague distrust at some sound or scent of one of the members of my party. And even as I considered these points, my neighbours the monkeys were doing the same with more experience to guide them and better equipment in the way of senses. They listened, considered, and understood, and I could hear their sub-human voices discussing the news.

Then, still far away, though nearer than the sambhur, I heard the shrill belling of the spotted deer as their herd turned all eyes and ears and noses to point to the approaching danger, so it was no challenge to a stag; but still the monkeys discussed it without emotion. Nearer came the cause of warning, itself silent amid noise. A little muntjac barked hoarsely and incessantly, his voice more like a dog's than the bell of a deer; and soon another took up the scent and joined in; and the squirrels helping in the chain of signals, whistled shrilly from their trees just round the bend; and from that we knew, the monkeys and I, that the danger was not man. They grew more alive to the danger's imminence. Outlying members moved inwards towards the company of the tribe, until all had gathered on the dome of one old tree, where they sat in groups and listened, and looked down the bed of the stream. Whether it was scent that gave first evidence to confirm their fear, or sound, or sight, I cannot tell; but all at once they seemed to know that the enemy was in their presence, and uplifted their voices in loud scandal, just as their descendants, our ancestors, might have shouted insults at the sabre-toothed tiger.

Then I, too, saw fear embodied, as a leopard walked slowly and deliberately up the bed of the stream. He was so dignified and calm that I almost blushed for my shameful relatives as he scorned their plebeian clamour with aristocratic contempt. If I did not actually blush then, I have since, for my disgraceful intention to murder an animal so noble. Bright, and clean, and exceedingly beautiful he looked, and as he came near I could see the easy power of the muscles moving inside his sleek skin as their noiseless pistons bore him onward poised in perfect grace. Presently he looked up at the vulgar frightened monkeys—they ought perhaps to be regarded as the bravest of the brave who stayed behind as a rearguard; but when he saw that they were out of reach he paid no more attention to them whatsoever, but halted, and looked slowly and carefully up the stream-bed and along each bank. My bower of shrubbery hid me from his penetrating gaze, but it also prevented me from bringing my rifle to bear in his direction, and I sat as harmless and immobile as a stone image of Buddha while the lovely creature dug a shallow basin in the sand and stood with his fore-paws in it, to cool them I thought at the time. Then once again he stared slowly and piercingly into the woods. His glance did not pass along in one movement, but it seemed rather that he looked at successive spots in turn, as I have seen Kapurala and other true foresters look piece by piece into the circle of jungle surrounding us, while I have been conscious that my own glance only swept its surface. So did the leopard look into and not at the woods on either side of the stream. I saw his intent glance directed upon a spot next to me, and I froze even to the extent of holding my eyelids from blinking. Then his searchlight beam of scrutiny moved one unit, and his eyes looked into mine. I could see how intelligent he was, and how utterly untameable; and then in one sudden movement his spring was released, and his body shot across the sand, low to earth, black and yellow and bright in the evening sunlight, and he fled into the forest. A moment later the monkeys and squirrels a furlong away had taken up their part in the warning signals, and I heard fear pass away into the distance even as I had heard it approach.

Crestfallen at what now rejoices me, I returned to camp and found Kapurala there, and the tale he told was a curious one. A good many miles away there was a hillock of rock, a sort of island in the sea of waving tree-tops, and a deep fissure in it held water even in the driest weather. Kapurala had been there to study tracks and get the news of the jungle, and to his amazement had found the water-hole tenanted by an elephant who had fallen in and been unable to get out again. Kapurala thought the news would have spread into the forest around, and did not expect other animals would come there to drink, so if sport was my object he advised me to stay where I was. But I preferred the live wonder to any prospect of trophies, and the next afternoon we set out for the water-hole.

We were four—Kapurala, two Tamils, and I. The walk was a long one, as it often proves when the miles are estimated by tireless men of the jungle; and the Sinhalese mile is in any case a measure of time, not of distance. It is the distance a man may march in a Sinhalese hour, which is twenty-four of our minutes, and measured thus it may be a four-mile walk to the top of a hill and only two miles back again, or five miles to a tracker and seven to a coolie with a load. The sun was low before we reached the outskirts of the rocks and began to tread silently in Kapurala's tracks. Not far back we had crossed the track of a solitary elephant, and Kapurala had muttered 'tusker' as he pointed out that the shape of the forefeet was more oval than commonly; but we did not see the animal, and now we were stepping in the footprints of a leopard who had gone our way an hour or so before. His track led right up to the rock, and then we looked for him no more, for a strange sight engaged our thoughts.

We stood at the edge of the forest and saw a long slope of rock falling from the right, where it merged into a boulder-strewn fold of the earth, to an abrupt fall on the left, where the rock ended like a revetment wall with a wooded hollow below it. The rock was black, and its slope not too steep to walk upon easily with rope-soled shoes. At highest it did not overtop the trees of the surrounding forest, and it was not more than an acre in extent. End on to our view as we stood, a fissure had split the rock across its slope much as a crevasse splits a glacier, and in the cleft thus formed green water made a pool some fifty feet long and about a quarter of that width. In the pool stood the elephant facing us. On his left, the wall of the pool rose too high for his trunk quite to reach, but on his right, as he stood knee-deep gazing at us, the rock wall came lower than the upper part of his breast, and it seemed so impossible that he should be unable to get out when he wished that I hesitated to advance. But Kapurala, who had been near him the day before, pointed to the droppings of the herd, and said the animal had been where he was not less than three days.

When we drew near the hole, the elephant charged its length and menaced us with his trunk; but the limitation of his movements soon grew plain, and we went freely up to within a few feet of his utmost reach. I saw then what a dangerous trap the hole had become. The margin on the lower side, where tens of thousands of generations of animals must have drunk, had been made smooth as glass, polished by their feet; the approach sloped down very steeply, and when the water had sunk low, thirsty beasts had to stoop farther and farther with neck outstretched until at last they could only drink in peril of sliding in. Whether the elephant had slid in thus, despite the advantage his trunk gave him, or whether he had been jostled in by the herd as they drank eagerly, we could not guess. There he was, and in no way could he get out. The pool tapered at its two ends and gradually became too narrow for the elephant to walk there with his broad feet, and he had tried to take advantage of this, levering himself up as a climber in a 'chimney,' with his feet thrust against one wall and his rump against the other. We could see the whitish patch worn on his buttocks by the repeated friction of the rock, and while we stood there he tried it once more, and failed again, for even the stimulus of his fury when we drew near could not win for him the extra foot he had to climb. We mounted the steep slope above, and I laid my rifle on the rock, and stood above the water-hole looking down upon the elephant. He knew he could not reach me there, and soon abandoned any effort to do so; and perhaps many animals may have stood where I did, in the last three days, and looked down upon him with wonder in their eyes, or with hunger, or thirst, but not with the pity I felt, though surely there must be a germ of it in animals or it could scarcely have developed in us. Perhaps one may see it in the eyes of a dog whose master is ill.

We had no axe, but I sent the three men into the forest to see what they could do with knives to lop off branches of the wild fig-trees elephants are fond of eating, and while they were in the woods I walked round the rock to observe more carefully where the game paths came in. It is always well to do this before nightfall, for when the sun sets, and the moon rises, and the shadows swing from east to west of their substantive forms, the whole scene may suffer a change so complete that landmarks may be lost, and animals come upon one unawares from unexpected angles. Twice I have known men shoot and hit the shadows of rocks believing them to be bears, for they had dozed, and when they awoke the shadow forms had altered, and to straining eyes seemed to be moving.

A game path came down from the right, between the boulders on the slope, and there was another opposite to that we had come in by, but for the rest of its circumference the rock fell away abruptly and there were no roads. My rifle was still lying above the pool, for, like Kapurala, I did not think animals would come to drink while the elephant was there, and on the bare rock there were no tracks to help me. But I had forgotten the leopard whom we had followed along the path, and looking over the rock on the far side I found him. He lay but a score of feet away, and his head turned up in swift inquiry as mine appeared above the edge of the little hill. Then, without due haste, he rose and loped lightly away into the shadow of the trees. He did not appear much afraid, and I incline to think he had heard us all along, and disregarded our talk as the chattering of monkeys. Maybe he had not known of men before, and our scent was blowing in the other direction; but in any case leopards often surprise one by their boldness, and their steps are pursued so commonly by a din of warning cries that they may have become inured to chattering noises such as men make.

I returned to find Kapurala dragging forth branches from the jungle, and like boys above a bear pit, we threw down a branch for the hungry elephant to eat. He did not even consider the matter; for his thoughts were concentrated upon more urgent things, and to him the branch was nothing but an object he could use to consolidate the mud beneath him so as to gain another step toward freedom. The first branch, and all others we gave him, he thrust beneath his feet and trod into the deep mud. It was clear that we had only to cut a few logs for him to build a platform and win his liberty; but whether he would not then have made it his first business to hunt us, his benefactors, was more doubtful, and Kapurala thought he would. In any case we had no axe, and something else happened to divert our thought from the elephant's troubles to our own.

The new turn of the wheel brought to pass so peculiar a position that I tremble lest by telling the whole truth I may become known as a writer of fairy stories. Nevertheless I shall tell it. Out from the boulders behind us as we faced the elephant marched three bears. It is true that one was small, but that only enhances the resemblance to Grimm. We had no way to retreat, for if the bears of Scylla were above us, the Charybdis of the elephant yawned more terribly below; for who could doubt that our fate, had we been driven into the water-hole, would have been that of the branches? Without anger or malice aforethought the hard-pressed giant would have built our bodies into his platform, and consolidated the mud with our bones.

I picked up my rifle, and the other men stood fast. One of them had my cartridge-bag slung on his shoulders, and I had only the two charges in the breech. They stood fast while I aimed, and they stood fast while I missed atrociously. I fired again, and the largest bear fell down, but in an instant was up again, and for a moment those three rough brave beasts stood puzzling it out and staring at the four of us. With an empty rifle I felt suddenly how useless it would be to strike downward when they charged, for the blow would certainly glance, and like a batsman who makes his vital decision in the second or two a cricket ball takes to travel the length of the pitch, I determined to play forward so as to bring the weight of my heavy barrels full against the first bear's nose. Then the bears turned and fled. To fail to follow up a wounded animal is unforgivable, and I did my best to follow that one; but inside the jungle it was already dark, and I lost the blood trail at once. It was thin, and I hope my second shot was almost as clean a miss as the first.

We now held a council of war, and I have never known Kapurala more anxious. I think we were all feeling that the jungle had rather a lot of surprises in it. We had no ready-made shelter to retire to, and it was too late to build a platform in a tree. The beasts are coming to the circus, said one of the men, and there will be a crowd; and a suggestion was made that we might retire into the woods and build a fire. But we all wanted to see the circus, so we built ourselves a little fort and stayed where we were.

The Sinhalese habitually use these forts, as they call them, but they do not as a rule leave it until a few minutes before dark sets in to start building them. It was some days after full moon, so we had several hours of pitch darkness to expect before the moon rose, and we worked like slaves to build for ourselves a horse-shoe wall some two feet high whose ends abutted upon the steep edge of the rock where we did not expect animals would try to climb. But Kapurala still felt genuine concern lest some fierce beast—leopard, or elephant, or bear—might blunder over our wall unawares and run amok in surprise and terror. There may have been some danger, though less than he felt at the time; but he was so vastly more experienced than I was, and of such proven courage, that I felt his advice had to be taken, and through the hours of darkness we sang in turn, like Orpheus, but to charm the animals away from us.

Kapurala was a Sinhalese, and the coolies were Tamils. They sang in their respective tongues, and I in mine; and the captive giant surged to and fro in his wet prison, beat upon the rock with his trunk, and from time to time trumpeted his vast sorrow to the stars.

When the moon rose we men grew quiet, but the elephant's restless movements never ceased; he churned the muddy water with his feet, and in our silence his tremendous trumpet echoed the farther over the solemn forest.

It was about midnight that the first visitor came, and as he clambered up a steep place on the far side, beyond the water-hole, I heard the click and scratch of claws that told me he was a bear. Soon we saw him as a black shadow that moved about the rock, silently now, for several minutes before he went near the hole to drink; but when he approached the brink, the elephant threatened him with his trunk, and would not let him. As he had menaced us, so did he menace the bear, making no difference whatsoever. The bear went wide of him, and tried to reach the opposite end of the pool; but the elephant swung round and drove him off once more. Again and again the bear tried to drink, but the guardian of the pool was inexorable, and did not relax his vigilance for one single minute; so the poor thirsty beast gave it up at last, and started, I suppose, to walk the dry miles that lay between him and our river-bed, for there was no water nearer. Yet even that is not certain; for, as the night wore on, no less than three times did other bears, or this bear returning, try to drink from the hole, and the elephant permitted none of them to succeed.

It was noticeable that none of the porcupines of the neighbouring rocks came to drink, for they are far commoner than bears, and drink freely from the same water-holes; but I suppose they do not go so far for their food or water, and those of the rocks around us had already learned that it was useless.

Between the visits of the bears the elephant never ceased his miserable patrol, and his lamentations shook the heavens until they so saddened me that I felt this immensity of sorrow was too vast for us all to bear, and I longed for the poor animal to die. Before dawn a bear came who ran right round the hole, and close by our fort I shot him; and after that no more creatures came before we left after taking his skin at sunrise.

All that remains to be told is the fate of the elephant. Immediately I got home the facts were reported, and a Sinhalese chief went down with tame elephants to extricate the prisoner. But the poor thing died. The struggle had been too much for him; and I suppose the bears, and the leopards, and the pigs, and the wild cats and jackals he had driven away from the water, gathered and ate of his great carcass until all of it had gone back to the forest that had nourished it for so long, until at last the porcupines crept into the hole and gnawed there such bones as they were unable to drag away, and the elephant's last debt was paid.

It is worth mentioning that a year or two later, in another water-hole in the same province, a cow elephant with her calf was found in like predicament. But this time their rescue was accomplished safely by a chief who set trained elephants to tame them where they were captive before building a platform and releasing them. As they are very valuable animals, he reaped the just reward of his sagacity.

A LEOPARD

The sun sank low behind the forest's rim,
As night brought peace to the aisles of the ancient wood,
Where sleeping trees in clustered columns stood
Upholding their temple's roof. Their forms loomed dim,
Save twigs' fine tracery, black upon western glow.
Silent were birds; the silent shades below
Lay lapped in dreams, and scent from an evening flower.

Then suddenly uprose the voice of power.
Grim and relentless, echoing far and deep
From rock to tree; calling aloud that war
Not yet may lull its restless soul to sleep;
For death through haunted tangles still must creep,
Lest life may lose its own most secret core.

VIII. WATER-HOLES

In all that great part of Ceylon where the sou'-west monsoon rains do not fall, water governs men and beasts alike, for, over hundreds of square miles, tanks and water-holes are the only places where they can drink for several months of the year. For fifteen centuries or more, each town lay beneath the bund of a large tank, and every village below a smaller one. The capital city was almost surrounded by tanks great and small, and one may infer that its position was chosen because the surrounding levels made this possible. But when prosperity swung over to the other side of the hills, the jungle tide rose over the kingdom, and age-old water-holes once more regained the importance they hold between the periods of civilisation, and held for thousands of centuries before tanks existed.

When the scorching wind rushes through the woods for months on end, and papery leaves rustle harshly on wiry twigs; when every footfall in the forest is betrayed by the crunching of its parched carpet; when soil in hollows that once were ponds grows brick hard, and deep cracks chequer the baked mud where footprints of the last beasts to seek water there remain cast as though in cement until again dissolved by October rains, seemingly unimportant clefts among the rocks assume strategic value, and direct the movements of wild animals, and even of men.

After walking for miles through an empty forest where even insect life seems depressed, it is astonishing to find little colonies of birds living round rock-holes. Some of them are visitors from the hills, whose migrant habits have been copied by European women; for the lovely paradise fly-catcher who nests in some garden in the nor'-east monsoon can be found passing the sou'-west as a visitor to a water-hole. Others are permanent forest dwellers, like the beautiful long-tailed robin whose song is the sweetest in all Ceylon, and another rather rare little bird who often owns a water-hole to himself, the three-toed kingfisher, whose gay habit it is to have rosy plumage where most of his tribe have blue.

In the hills it is the fords, the passes, and the ridges that have preordained the system of the elephants' roads; but in the wide forests of the plain the animals' paths are linked to water-holes as nodes or junctions whence they radiate in all directions into the woods, there to split into an infinity of ramifications that meander on until they get lost among the leaves. But the scarcely visible track, if persistently followed, may soon be found running into one a little more clearly defined, and that into another somewhat larger, until, by choosing of two ways ever the more worn, one may come in time to a hard-beaten deeply rutted path, a real animal highway that will lead to a water-hole.

The most enduring water-holes, with the sweetest water, are found in the outcrops of gneiss rocks in the plain. Commonly these slab rocks slope gently over an acre or more of unbroken surface, an ideal catchment area whereon the slightest shower of rain is received and drained off into some fault in the rock, deep, narrow, partly shaded, and able to retain water throughout the months of drought. Durable water-holes are found in all forms, but the commonest is shaped like a canoe, long and narrow, and is often of great depth.

All round the rock stands a circle of solemn trees, discreet witnesses of tragedies played in the little arena they encompass. They attain the full stature of their kind right up to the edge of the slab, and there stop dead, for on the rock itself, in scanty cracks filled by detritus, the place of the forest trees is taken by grey-green euphorbias, thorn-fringed prehistoric plants whose tortured branches bleed white blood when broken. From all sides the animals' roads come to the edge of the slab, and there generally end, for most beasts like to skirmish around before they care to drink; but the edge of the hole that the water lips when full is often worn smooth as the steps of a shrine by the feet of its worshippers, and on the brink strong animal odour is clamant even to the blunt senses of civilised man.

It seems instinctive with many to tread lightly near water-holes, observant of sounds and signs, for one never knows what eyes may be watching, or whose pointed ear may not be cocked to listen. I have often noticed the preference shown by the great grey wanderoo monkeys for sitting on tree-tops where they get a distant view, on the sides of hills, or in high trees by the edges of tanks or fields, or on boughs overhanging rivers; and they love, too, to sit watching water-holes, quietly hidden among the leaves, only to reveal their presence after a while by some movement, or by uttering a word of their speech. May it not be that they find life entertaining there? A dog often enjoys spending his life by the gate, noticing all who pass, and barking at those he disapproves of. Working women gossiping on door-steps, old gentlemen sitting in club windows, and monkeys perched on high boughs by water-holes are less dissimilar than they suppose. The hunter scouting for news of game makes for a water-hole to study the tracks, and often gathers information there of men whose footprints are familiar to him, as well as of public characters among the animals such as dangerous rogue elephants, or, near villages, notorious cattle-killing leopards. The wandering animals, buffaloes, leopards, and bears, better foresters than men, must often pick up at water-holes news of their friends and enemies, and the trail of lovers they have lost and would seek again; and the deer bell piteously the old story of the leopard who watches the pass. All roads in Europe are said to lead to Rome, and in Ceylon's dry plain all animal roads lead to water-holes.

Sometimes elephants come in herds and drink small holes dry. I was on my way to a hole late one afternoon when we struck a deeply rutted game track that led through sombre forest where black boulders, large as houses, strewed the earth in the gloomy shade of old palu and ebony trees. The path ran at length beside a little cliff, the perpendicular flank of a high rock dome that raised its head up into the yellow light of the slanting sun; but in the shades below it was nearly dusk, and in my rope-soled shoes I almost walked on to a leopard who sat at the foot of the rock eating a muntjac deer. Before I was in a position to fire the leopard glided behind the serpentine folds of a multiple-stemmed creeper, and stayed peering through at me with curious eyes. I edged to the left to outflank him, but he did likewise, and we waltzed half round the tangle before he changed his tactics and disappeared into the shades, leaving to me as the more formidable beast the venison he had killed. We went on, and a few hundred yards farther came to the water-hole we sought. It was a small hole, and there was no water in it. One end ran into the rock for a little way like a tunnel, a not unusual formation. All around it were tracks left by the muddy feet of elephants, and large piles of their droppings made the place smell like a stable. The footmarks were of many sizes, and though I was unable to unravel the number of the herd, it had at least been numerous and thirsty enough to drink the rock-hole dry. After the elephants had left, wild pigs had clambered down into the pit, and furrowed the mud that remained ; for this hole was easy of access, and not a trap for thirsty animals, and I was surprised to see in the ploughed-up mud the antlers of deer, the skull of a pig, and other unidentified bones. Had these been accessible when fresh they would have been eaten, and it was plain that their owners had met death while the hole was full of water. But how? They were not shot, or their slayers would have dragged them out. It was possible they had been struck on the brink by leopards and had fallen in and died, but it seemed very unlikely ; it might happen once, but not several separate times. I think a crocodile must have been the author of the problem. At some time one must have made this hole his retreat for the dry weather, and these were the relics of wretched creatures he had dragged in and buried in the mud. This is not so unlikely as it may appear, and is probably not very uncommon. I sat one night close to a water-hole, keeping studious watch on the shadows where the game paths led out into the moon-light. Each rustling leaf found me alert, with eyes probing the entries of the woods. but never a thought did I give to the water-hole itself until a crocodile suddenly dragged itself over the stone lip, and ran across the rock into the safe shadows of the forest. To the common perils of approach this horror was added, and though I suppose their senses would warn them of his lurking presence, some more daring or foolish among animals half-crazed with thirst had taken the risk, and paid the price of death, the only price the jungle will receive as full payment for error. Crocodiles have few effective foes save men with guns, unless it be their own kind or their parasites, but once I found one who had died a violent death at the hands of his selected victim. He lay dead in a water-hole in the loneliest forest I know, floating belly uppermost, his white under side slashed by four parallel gashes evidently ripped by a leopard's powerful hind claws. His presence poisoned the water, and perhaps the brave leopard had won free only to creep away and die; but I rejoiced that the jungle should contain a justice not less blind and inexorable than any figure carved to adorn men's courts of law. Yet, feeling so, what must I think of men who sat by water-holes to kill thirsty bears? What of myself, who had often done so? If these questions the jungle asks are faced honestly, they are not easy to evade or to answer. There is, I think, this in mitigation, that some men give up killing before they give up watching wild animals. While young they fulfil the hunting instincts that grew in man while his race was yet in its youth, but later they extend to wild animals who have not bowed to our yoke part of the mercy they give naturally to those who have submitted to our commandments and become tame. Crocodiles, on the other hand, kill to their dying day; but as a counter to that argument, crocodiles kill only for food, and men for the love of it; and I think the day of judgment would find crocodiles armed with the better evidence in their favour.

The water-hole was dry, and we thought no more of sitting by it, but sought instead for some comfortable place where we might pass the night in peace; and just before sunset we found a way to climb the tall rock at whose foot lay the remnants of the deer. The moon was full, and when she had risen well above the trees I could see for miles over the forest. The leaves twinkled at me, but I could not penetrate their screen, and the ground was so hidden from me that when the leopard came back to renew his feast, I could not get a glimpse of him, although I could hear the dead deer's bones crack in his jaws.

A curious part of the stock of knowledge that comes under the general heading of woodcraft is gained from studying dung. Swift, I recall, wrote an essay on it, and one need not hesitate to follow a dean. It is most revealing, and I have no doubt that animals themselves get much information from its observation, as, indeed, no one can doubt who has watched them. On the heels of an elephant accounted dangerous, one may see a tracker, a jungle professor of woodcraft, thrust his bare foot into its giant droppings to estimate from the heat they retain how far ahead the animal is likely to be. The rock we had selected for our rest-house was not easy to climb, and its weather-worn surface, steep, and exposed to sun and wind and rain, was not one to retain footprints; but a short walk round it before the sun set sufficed to tell us that a variety of animals frequented its bare slopes and hard summit. Mongooses had been there, and many porcupines, and even more monkeys, and one leopard at least. I suspect the monkeys were the original cause of the mountaineering. For many hours after the sun has ceased shining rocks retain heat, and monkeys like to sit where it is warm; moreover, they could look out over the world, and if danger came upon them suddenly could leap down with outstretched arms to the tree-tops below; and one of their tree roads connected with their road across the rock. In their droppings are often to be found undigested nuts and seeds that might account for the porcupines' enterprise, while perhaps the larvæ of dung-rolling beetles might attract the mongooses, or more likely they had roamed in mere curiosity, for they are keen exploring beasties. The leopard had, of course, come after the monkeys; and we who came for a quiet night, and to listen to the jungle, gathered all this additional knowledge, not without interest, from these humble relics. After all, the study of animals' movements in an evergreen forest is largely an affair of clues and inferences, and the same qualities that would go to the making of a successful detective are valuable to a tracker. Of all the evidence possible, a good view of the animal comes first, of course, but it is perhaps the rarest. Tracks come next, and close on their heels come sounds; while scent is a rare accomplishment, and must rank after the study of dung as a road to knowledge.

Some hours after the moon rose I heard a

shrill voice complaining in miserable tones. From somewhere beneath the black and silver surface of the forest a plaintive wailing rose, inexpressibly fine drawn by distance, a thin thread of sound, but soon it came nearer, and then I could hear another voice, the gruff tones of a she-bear comforting her baby. They were following in my footsteps towards the water-hole, and a few minutes later I heard their feet pad softly along the path where it skirted the foot of my rock! Whether the leopard was still sitting over his supper I do not know; in any case, the bears did not turn aside, but padded steadily on towards the hole, and I heard the cub cry as they passed away. I knew the disappointment they were doomed to, and in the voice of the baby there seemed tragedy as they left that useless hole and went on into the dark wilderness to seek water. To know even a little of the animals' point of view makes one ponder very deeply over the triumph of our race over the others. Are we altogether so glorious a species as we suppose? The fiercest enemy these wild creatures once knew was the leopard, whose hunger was but a selective agent, one of evolution's forces; but now man is the exterminator of hunted and hunting beasts alike. It is not lack of admiration for enterprise that makes me feel myself on the side of the animals in this long war, but pity for the utter helplessness of the hunted.

The leopard below the rock lived to boast that he had looked in the eyes of a man and come off unscathed; and once I lived to make the complementary claim twice within twelve hours. I had sat in a tree with a broad easy trunk on a platform of sticks like a wood-pigeon's nest, armed with a light repeating rifle that enabled me to pump out twelve little bullets in about twice that number of seconds. It was a ridiculously inadequate weapon, but I was too inexperienced to know the danger, and too ignorant to appreciate the cruelty of using such a toy against fighting animals. My tree sprang from the foot of an uprising rock, in whose side a deep crevice held water at the same level as my seat; so when a leopard came and sat like a big cat by the tiny pool, his eyes were even with mine; and when he turned his head and looked at me, he saw me in the shadow as clearly as I saw him out there in the brilliant moonlight. I saw his keen face look inquiringly at me, and then I fired, for I feared he might suddenly flee. My shot hit him high in the chest, and without the smallest halt or hesitation he charged down the rock and ran up my tree as a cat runs up a wall. I stood up and worked the little rifle like a machine-gun, and at a range closing very swiftly from ten or twelve feet to less than one yard I shot four more of my small bullets into his chest, and then he dropped and died. My tame leopards often rushed up easy trees like that in play, but that was the nearest vision I ever had of fierce eyes glaring while the brain behind them longed furiously to get to grips before it died. On my side there was no fear then, for the action was too swift for the birth of any emotion foreign to the immediate struggle; and that encourages the hope that the leopard suffered no more than a back who falls on the ball before the charging pack and saves a try. The body of the leopard lay immediately beneath me, and again I sat in silence and waited for the forest to usher forth more of its children; and after some hours another leopard came, and this time I fired before he had seen me. Bright, low to the rock, and marvellously swiftly the leopard fled. I heard him crash twice in the undergrowth, and then there was silence; and though we listened intently we were not quite sure we heard him again. When morning came, my old tracker, Kapurala the wise, crawled into the thicket with me, and we set out on the blood trail.

It is a paradoxical and very curious fact that many people find strange pleasure in fear, not always and everywhere, but as an occasional phenomenon. I was horribly afraid, and yet would not have been elsewhere for almost any reward. The leopard had chosen a rocky line to travel, and not much was to be seen but here and there a spot of blood, and occasionally a footprint on a soft patch of sand; so we crept on by inches, often stopping to listen and stare into the bushes, and presently Kapurala pointed to a tiny smear of blood on a leaf that showed the wound was high and perhaps not very dangerous. Once we crossed a more open area where the track led across sand with even stride and no sign of limp; and then the blood took us into a thicket of thorny shrubs, and we had to creep once more. I had discarded my rifle and taken a shotgun; and when we came out of the thorns into the dry bed of a little water-course we saw the leopard in front of us. He lay full length on a rock that sloped away from us, and all we could see were the higher portions of his body and half of his head. He lay so still that I thought he was dead until an ear twitched; and then he heard us, and sat up suddenly, and turned and looked down at my face. I thought he would charge like the other, and judged it best to wait for a very close shot; but his decision was different, and after one long stare he sprang lightly down on the far side and disappeared. A moment later monkeys cried out frantically in a tall tree a hundred yards beyond, and before they had stopped their clamour another troop of their brothers much farther away took up the alarm and shouted at the fugitive passing beneath their tree; so we knew the leopard was not badly injured, and that pursuit had become fruitless.

Like all experiences that carry a man far from himself, sitting at night by a water-hole is fascinating enough to gild its morality, for it takes one back a very long journey to listen to the sounds of a kingdom wherein human beings have no place except as intruders; but it needs good understanding of the things heard to get from those sub-human voices the full value of their message. Sometimes it is only small beasts who rustle, and peep, and come scurrying over the rock to their drink, little jungle cats, jackals, and often porcupines; small beasts when weighed, but when a porcupine approaches a dangerous pass with every quill erect he looks a foot higher and wider than he really is, for in the *chevaux-de-frise* he carries round him some spikes are not less than fifteen inches long. Many a man has shot at a porcupine by moonlight and thought he was firing at a bear; and some have been rather difficult to convince of their optimism, for if the night be cloudy it is really very difficult to tell; but though a bear may snuffle like a porcupine, and though both may breathe heavily, it is generally possible to hear the rustle of quills, or to make out, however faintly, the white patch on a porcupine's stern.

Once, when I was sitting with ever-wise

Kapurala, we heard a crash and a choked cry, almost a scream, which made eerie signal from the darkness that it was the voice of death. With his mouth against my ear, the old man whispered, "It is a leopard who leaps on a deer!" And soon we heard the grumble of a leopard in the wood hard by, and next his harsh roar, like a cross-cut saw rending a hard log. My mentor thought there were two leopards, for the roaring was intermittent for several hours; but they did not come into view, and all we knew of the tragedy was its sound until we went and found the dead deer at dawn.

Another time it was a comedy that was acted in the woods close by, and signalled to us by its incidental music. It began with a yelp, and went on with barks and yells, and an appalling cacophony like the mixture of a naughty nursery with a big dog-fight. Again Kapurala whispered, "It is bears who make love!" and he chuckled. "Soon they will be thirsty and come to drink." And he was right, for after a spell the furious sounds ended, and two bears came out together and drank peacefully side by side. I put up my rifle and drew a bead first on one and then on the other as he stood waiting for his comrade to finish her drink; but I did not fire, and they went off together into the shadows with my blessing, and never knew it.

These strong animals, fierce and fearless in their pride, seldom betray timidity in approaching water unless the locality is one persecuted by hunters, and even then if the hunters they have known are Tamil or Sinhalese, not of the boot-wearing kind, they do not greatly fear. The village hunter shoots leopards near home, for they menace his herd, but in more remote jungles he has but one aim in spending money on powder, and that is to get its value in meat. He will slay deer, old or young, stag or hind, in season and out of season, and by any means; but he often collects a little pile of stones beside him in ambush by a water-hole so that he may throw them at animals whose presence there will scare away his bread-winning deer. There is a Government reward for killing leopard or bear, but it does not pay so well as an undisturbed trade in meat. Bears generally go fairly directly to their drink, but leopards are more leisurely animals, fonder of taking thought, and more prone to hark to the sounds the night wind brings them, and to wonder. When a leopard turns his head towards some voice of the woods, it is obvious he considers its message, and he appears far less self-centred than a bear, and more aware of lives other than his own. It is true his philosophy is strict utilitarianism, but so often is ours, and his is at least virile. Perhaps man may be the dull animal he is at worst because he did not pass into the hunting stage until his bodily form and the chief folds in his brain were already fixed.

I have found it almost more interesting to watch deer come to water than the forceful beasts, particularly the tall and wary sambhur who do not go in herds like spotted deer, and are more individual in consequence. Sometimes they come alone, but more often, I think, in families. Some stags will stay close to a pool for hours before daring to drink, trying this side and that, and walking out into the moonlight at the edge of the forest only to melt once again into the shadows, where they are as invisible as the proverbial black cat in a dark room. Sometimes a stag is silent, barely betrayed to the most instructed ear by an occasional sliding pebble, or the rasp of hoof on rock, or the brush of a leaf along his side. At others he will bell with bugle challenge, and stamp his forefoot so as to produce a whirring vibratory sound as though the earth itself trembled, and exactly how this is caused I have never fathomed. At last, with trumpet ears ever turning, and with many pauses, he will come slowly down, drink deep, and go in silence; or he may take heart to run in hastily, and then, before more than tasting the water, gallop off in panic, and with a crash of the undergrowth dissolve once more into the silent, watchful, listening, fearing forest. When on Gallipoli we had to fill our water-bottles at springs measured and marked by snipers, we knew the sambhur's inner thoughts.

It is natural that caves should often be found associated with water-holes, and where that occurs it is generally possible to discern some trace of monastic occupation in the centuries that lie between the third B.C. and the sixth A.D. There are some wonderful groups of rocks where whole ranges of caves look out upon the water-holes, and annexed to them are the ruins of buildings proper to monasteries: schools, refectories, temples, and the like. Some of these draw pilgrims and tourists, but many others are hardly visited by men other than village hunters once in ten years, and there seems no reason above the horizon at present why they should be. One such little town among the rocks I know where a later culture already lies superimposed upon the age of Buddhism that ended, so far as the inscriptions tell one, about fourteen centuries ago. After the monks had gone, and jungle had come back full tide, Veddhas had dwelt in the caves, and had drawn in colours on the walls pictures of hunting scenes most rudely outlined, and diagrammatic pictures of gods or heroes, and replicas of their tribal symbol, the bow with arrow placed on string. They have gone, and the Veddhas who went with me there do not know anything about them, and have no reverence for the caves; but in a water-hole there someone has planted a lotus, and when I saw its white bloom in the dark hole among the black rocks I wondered that a jungle hunter should have created such unexpected beauty in that abandoned place out of unmixed love of its loveliness.

Another notable place where there are water-holes and caves in association lies within a mile of a much frequented rest-house, but no one ever finds it, and I shall not say where it is. Many centuries ago a very large monastery straggled up a rocky hill where scores of caves were inhabited by monks; and in one of the largest of these a great image of Buddha, more than twenty feet from head to heel, was built close to the rock at the back of the cave, probably in the sixth century A.D. Now all has gone back to the forest except one small cave at the foot of the hill that is still used as a temple by the two poor and fever-stricken monks who remain to represent a powerful community. I have read them the inscriptions cut in the rock above their temple's roof, for they have not the skill to do so. Behind their cave forest stands unbroken, and bears come down to the monks' back door. One may still pursue the flight of steps that runs upward through the woods, though with difficulty, for forest has grown over it for a thousand years. By caves and boulders the steps lead to the foot of a vast overhanging rock, huge as the hull of an Atlantic liner, and leaning out to form the roof of a long cave, never more than forty feet wide, but ten times that in length. In old days this long covered way was divided into compartments by stone walls, with the temple of the image at the end of all, beside the water-hole; and even now crumbling remnants of the partitions still cut it into cubicles, whose floors are of soft dust dotted with the footprints of many animals who have walked or lain there. The dust is fine as flour, and I have seen its surface crawl with ticks that have fallen from the animals who use it for their bed. In so protected a place it is difficult to judge the age of tracks, and all the animals whose record is imprinted there have obviously come in succession and not together; for it is usual to see in one or other of the little rooms the tracks of bears, leopards, sambhur, pigs, jackals, and porcupines; and if one of these is missing when I guide someone to this extraordinary place, I am disappointed. Between the long figure of Buddha and the rock a dark tunnel runs. It is open at both ends now, but may have been a treasure chamber at some remote time, for in a cave of equal age I was once taken secretly behind a similar image and shown some old ivory tusks. But now this dark corridor is a favourite promenade for leopards, whose fresh tracks are seldom wanting; and before peering in it is wise to throw a stone from a distance so as to give the animal time to escape and let you see the image without diversion. Few indeed among wild animals will attack unprovoked unless come upon so closely and suddenly that they think they cannot escape. The water-hole by the temple is a cistern cut in the stone by artificers of two thousand years ago if it be as old as the earliest writings on the boulders. Beside it is carved an inscription as yet not deciphered in letters of about the sixth century A.D. This place can almost be reached by car, and yet it remains unknown, and thinking upon this, I take hope for that other little town with its white lotus amid the rocks so wild and deserted, and pray that it may hold hard to its lonely beauty for thousands of years to come.

So these water-holes by the caves have their own interesting history, but I incline to think that where there are no caves the holes may prove some day to be the custodians of a history much more remote and unexplored. Their examination has not yet begun, and my hopes may be disappointed, but there are reasons for them. Where there have been monasteries it is probable that all the water-holes have been dug out clean and dry at least once, and the mud that now lies in them will contain nothing older than fragments of the monk's pottery; but in those water-holes where no monks have lived there may be relics of very much earlier periods. Since the season of drought is the south-west monsoon, the hunters' ambushes are generally on the opposite side of the pool; but not always, for unexpected eddies in the wind are caused by rocks or trees. When no trees stand within easy shot of the hole, and forty yards is a very long shot by moonlight, the hunters build little rock hiding-places they call 'forts' out of the boulders that lie around. These are sometimes round, sometimes square, and often formless; and I have sat in 'forts' an hour old, and in others I believe were built by stone age man. Now that the age of tanks has waned, and for as long as forest covers the deserted kingdom, water-holes will play their part in the affairs of animals. Bears may die out, and leopards become as rare as merciful men, but the holes where they drank will remain; and for the present, while the animals still exist in fair numbers, conditions may justly be compared with those that prevailed before tanks were built. Then, as now, the animals' roads led to water-holes, and were the highways of jungle hunters. Then, as now, men sat in ambushes and shot at thirsty deer, only with arrows instead of bullets. And then, as now, the wind blew from the south-west. The effective range of any weapon by moonlight is governed by visibility, and trajectory has nothing to do with it. I have seen a famous rifle-shot who had represented England at Bisley miss a standing leopard at twenty yards in the light of a misty moon; so I think the hunters of palæolithic times sat exactly where men sit now, and not improbably made better shots. The water-holes should contain arrow-heads as well as bullets; and the stone tips of spears used to finish wounded beasts; and not only weapons, but women's ornaments, drinking vessels, and perhaps even the fossils of human beings. For water-holes are sometimes dangerous traps. I have described how an elephant fell into one and eventually died there; and in another hole I found a dead bear. My taste runs not in the line of post-mortems, but I examined that bear and found no wound, while the lip was polished and the hole was deep. And in a water-hole on the top of a wind-blown hill I found a prisoner stranger perhaps than even these. It was an ancient cistern with perpendicular sides cut ten feet deep into the rock; and one stormy day when I could scarcely stand against the gale that tore over the bare hill-top, I found a hawk, the Indian peregrine falcon, floating on the water, still alive, but so clemmed with cold that he died despite all care, a hot blanket, and even a tot of whisky. From these observations I feel it safe to infer that water-holes of the best type, canoe-shaped, and deep, and free from monastic interference, are likely to contain evidence of Ceylon's pre-history more valuable than any sites yet explored.

I have not dug a water-hole, but I did make some search in several of the boulder 'forts,' and was rewarded by the discovery of chert and crystal flakes foreign to the rock they lay on, and certainly brought there by men. As to their age there was small evidence, for on solid rock they might lie for ever and sink no further in. It is quite possible, of course, that jungle men in Ceylon may have been using stone-tipped arrows in comparatively modern times, although at Sigiriya, a fortress at its zenith in the sixth century A.D. and abandoned before the twelfth, not only was iron used abundantly, but steel tools were unearthed.

Water-holes that still contain water are not necessarily the most likely to contain relics of prehistoric man. I have known a great water-hole to spring a leak and run dry because a fig-tree found lodgment in its narrow end, and growing stoutly, split the rock. Many have silted up; and, however deep a hole, it must silt up in the long-run if it is never dug out; for dust, leaves, the detritus of weathering rock, and the animal droppings washed into it will ultimately fill it. There is no reason why a silted-up hole should not be as promising to excavate as one in active commission.

When one reflects how India has been invaded over and over again from lands to the northward, and when one considers the shape of India, tapering to a point as though formed for a funnel to fill Ceylon, and how races lose their vigour in the tropics and are driven forward by more vigorous northerners, it is difficult to resist the conclusion that Ceylon's water-holes hold the history of many invasions. The Straits are narrow and easily crossed, and there is no case of going on, for the next land to the south is the Antarctic.

Some water-holes are known to very few men, some to one only, for they are valuable property when kept secret. Rival hunters are feared, but I have known cunning men of the woods who were willing enough to take a Briton to their preserves by roundabout ways, like unjust taxi-drivers, though they would deny all knowledge when in the presence of their kind. For they knew I could not find my way back by a path deliberately made circuitous and baffling, unless I blazed a trail openly. Since jungle men often die sudden deaths, it must happen sometimes that holes are forgotten (and what more likely where cities have lost even their names?) and fall once more to the service of thirsty animals unmolested save by beasts of prey; and this gives them a chance to prosper, for the balance of the jungle is always more merciful than the destroying avarice of men.

EYES

WHO follow adventure must stare in the mirrors of death:
Strange eyes, they are sometimes, with always a secret behind,
Though hidden in fear or in wrath, like a leopard whose breath
Mingled mine where we fought in a tree, until suddenly blind
Went those searchlights of fury, and told me the fight had been gained;
For, scoring the bark as they slipped, his curved talons gave way
Till he fell to the earth with a thud, all his colour retained,
And the marvellous curves of his muscular form where he lay.
So I laughed in the tree, as my forerunners laughed when they fought;
But grew silent and cold while I wondered what lacked to my joy;
For it might have been I who lay dead; and what else had I sought
But the skin of this creature to give to a girl for a toy!

I have looked in the eyes of a bear, little furious eyes,
Partly hidden, and piercing a tangle of ragged black hair:
Then she roared while she rushed, with her mouth gaping wide in surprise
At my look, and my smell that enraged her and tainted the air;

And the white of my smooth naked chest and the gleam
  of my arms,
Where I stood at the door of my tent under vertical sun,
But enraged her the further, till maddened with hate and
  alarms
She charged on, and came straight for my face in a swift
  awkward run,
With fangs shining white as I struck her, when swiftly her
  head
Turned to bite at the wound, as though that were the
  cause of her pain.
But a second shot plunged through her heart, and she
  crumpled up dead;
Just a robe of black fur on the leaves, and a sticky red stain.

I have stared in a buffalo's eyes, and was sickened by fear
As I followed through thorns on his trail, and crawled
  through the brake
With sweat running streams down my arms as I slowly
  drew near
To each thicket in turn, and could see and could feel my
  hand shake.
But the conquering force that compels and is master of
  men
Drove me on, and forbade me to halt, if my heart would but
  last
Through its clamorous thumping. For I saw there was
  froth in the blood,
And could hear the deep guttural grunt of a lung-smitten
  beast
Who was bound to swing round before long and come back
  like a flood,
Irresistibly onward till death loosed his knees and he
  stopped.
Then it happened. All suddenly. Out came a head through
  the thorns,

And his pain-maddened eyes glared in mine while I aimed.
Then he dropped ;
Ana I looked, and saw earth and not blood on the spears
of his horns.

Stranger mirrors than these have I seen, and their eyes
have found mine
The last vision they had of this earth before death claimed
his own.
For I crawled in the dark through a cave till I saw the
light shine
On the marbled grey eye of a crocodile hiding alone
In a hole where the earth kept the torturing sunlight at
bay.
For a second we stared : then I fired, and hot smoke filled
the den,
And I heard his death scurry, and laughed as I wriggled
away
Through the dust, to the light, and the birds, and the
voices of men.
But few thoughts can one read in the eyes of a reptile, or
learn
If he hates us, or fears, or is cognisant only of life ;
For a cobra I caught in my hand where he rose from the
fern
Never altered his eyes till he died and thus ended the strife

With my back to a bank, with the eyes of a foe fixed on
mine
While he waited an order, his bayonet swung ready to
thrust,
A tickle crept out of my stomach and ran up my
spine,
As I looked up the light on his blade and saw freckles of
rust.

Then I heard my own voice saying, " Strike for my heart, not down there ";
And most gravely he nodded his head, like a courteous knight,
Though he knew not a word of my tongue. And the day seemed so fair
It was hard to believe Charon's ferry-boat crossed to the night;
Nor felt I much fear, though the tickle had made me feel sick.
Then suddenly all this bright picture, eyes, sunlight, and steel,
Fell shivered in pieces, as though by a conjurer's trick,
And I moved on my feet, nor know yet what had brought the repeal.

IX. OLD TRAILS

DIM memories lie hid in our consciousness, and slink away from the light of full perception. They rarely come forward frankly to be recognised, and yet are perpetually present and seen by the corner of the eye. When we sleep the living ghosts of our own past, perchance of our race's, come lightly forth to people our dreams, and shine as do dull embers when the sunlight that killed their glimmer is withdrawn. So with races; for though in the rush of active development their sub-memories are overlooked, when they sleep these wake again, and glow once more till they seem as real as actual affairs of to-day.

In the forests of Lanka the people still sleep and dream of the past, and the figures that throng their dreams belong to a forgotten age when the Sinhalese nation had not yet been formed.

It is a commonplace to speak of the buried cities of Ceylon, but it is a kingdom that lies buried there among the roots of trees, and it may be dug into with other tools than pick-axes; for the beliefs of the people offer a wide avenue of approach to the culture of their prehistoric ancestors. How long this will remain open it is difficult to estimate. I do not suppose that even one person had foreseen the awakening of Asia, that is now a fact, so short a time ago as when I went east of Suez three years before the nineteenth century ended; and it may be that before another thirty years have gone by this avenue will be closed; but it is not closed yet. In the jungle, and in villages that were jungle-girt within the memory of their older inhabitants, religious practices, superstitions, charms, cures, and legends still survive that were old when the wave of Buddhist missionary enthusiasm swept down into southern Asia more than twenty-one centuries ago. Buddhist culture has sunk far below its highest level, pulled down in India by the jealousy of the Brahmins, overrun in Java by more zealous Islam, corrupted in Tibet, and in Ceylon drowned in the jungle tide that flowed over city and village, temple and monastery, until their very names were lost, and in the capital city vast monuments relatively as notable as St Paul's and Westminster Abbey exchanged their titles while no one knew. But the pre-Buddhist culture still swims, for it never pinned its faith to power and riches, it never built great shrines and monasteries, and it does not appear ever to have had an organised church. The jungle tide rose above all those strong things, but over the beliefs and practices woven into the lives of jungle people who were members of its own fauna it rose harmlessly, for they flourished in its depths, and still live there and in its outskirts. Sometimes it seems that all the good there is in any religion springs from the ideals of a single founder, but this is a religion without a founder known even to myth or legend, nor has it any prophet, or any martyr, or any supreme head either on earth or elsewhere. If in this way it lacks what cannot be supplied, in another way it is free of what other religions cannot cure themselves, for rancour and persecution and the jealousy of rival sects enter not at all into a faith which has no ecclesia.

It is curious to consider what are the qualities in men's works that give them power to survive, and it would be difficult to foretell which elements of our own, or any other civilisation, will persist for even one thousand years. Speaking in round figures, the Portuguese, the Dutch, and the British have each ruled over the lowlands of Ceylon for one and a half centuries. Of the political power of the Portuguese, who came first, no trace remains, and their descendants are assimilated and rank almost as a caste: the Dutch Burghers, who came second, still hold records of pedigrees that link them with Europe, and still have a political organisation that enables them to keep their interests before Government. Their traditions of behaviour remain European rather than Asiatic. The British still rule. Of Portuguese titles to land I believe none exist, though titles based upon documents granted by the Sinhalese kings who ruled before them are not rare, and titles supported by Dutch documents are common. The law of the land is still called Roman-Dutch, though, of course, it is profoundly modified by British enactments; but Portuguese law is mute. Yet the religion brought in by the Portuguese continues to be that of a very large section of the populace; while those branches of Christianity professed by the British have relatively few adherents, and the Dutch Church almost none. Portuguese music survives too, though the songs of the Dutch are dead; and while half a dozen persons have learned to read Dutch for special reasons, Portuguese is still spoken freely in the poorer quarters of several towns. Fate has for some reason picked for survival religion, language, and music from among the wisdom of the Portuguese; and law, household comfort, and family pride from the customs of the Dutch; and some future observer will doubtless note what is selected for survival from among the manifold ways of the British. To hazard a prediction, I would give my vote to cricket.

From pre-Sinhalese times very much still survives. Fossilised in the form of charms, actually living in the bodies of priests of the older culture, *kapuralas* and *anumetiralas*, who by assuming the garments or weapons of their god become the god himself, and in the wood-god worship, the pre-Buddhist religion has persisted through all the vicissitudes of the whole stormy history of the Sinhalese nation. In some parts of Ceylon, where forests are rapidly becoming a memory to the old and a tradition to the young, almost every village has somewhere within its borders a grove, a little bit of woodland left uncut and uncleared: it may be only a few perches in area, but it is the home of a god. No image is there, but in a tiny room is kept some garment, or an ornament, or a spear or sword, something that is the god's own property, and which his priest holds or wears when he becomes inspired and dances or utters prophecies in the god's name. The priest *is* the god for the time being, and nothing more utterly different from Buddhism could be devised; yet the people who worship, and the men who rank as priests, all profess and call themselves Buddhists, and are described as such in the census returns. I suspect these temples in groves to be closely allied to the wood-god worship of the forest, for their homes are still woods, if only a few yards square. In a score of ways these temples of the older gods differ more from Buddhism than Christianity does from its cousin Islam; but in none more than in their absolute freedom from ecclesiasticism. In the *vihara*, every Buddhist monk is a member of an order, a celibate by profession, and bound by strict rules of conduct written in many books, commented on, annotated, dissected, and wellnigh killed by formalism; but the priests of the older gods are free individuals, attached to no order, owning allegiance to no hierarch, hoping nothing from promotion; but marrying, working, and living the lives of ordinary villagers like anyone else except when occasion calls for the use of spiritual powers. The position is hereditary as a rule, not necessarily passing to the eldest son, but to him in whom is most plainly inherited the faculty of somnambulism, or self-induced trance, which enables him to assume the state believed to indicate that the god is incarnated in his body. It might be possible, and would if so be extraordinarily interesting to ascertain whether this subjective accomplishment follows the lines of mendelian probability in its descent.

The religion of the older gods has kept its character remarkably distinct, in spite of a very early compromise with Buddhism, whereby, in many instances, the *dewale*, or god's temple, is situated actually inside the temple of Buddha, separated sometimes only by a curtain. But in these cases I think the god is always one of the Hindu pantheon, himself enslaved by formalism, represented by a statue, and only remotely connected with the little imageless *dewcles* of the woods. To instance the complete informality of the older worship I may describe a place I know where motor omnibuses halt under a tree among whose branches is a small, open, wooden box, about big enough for a pair of pigeons to nest in. A few leaves are hung on twigs before it, and at night I have sometimes seen a little lamp lit, and that is all. It is the second most primitive form of shrine; the most primitive of all having the leaves, but not the box or lamp.

I think the people of the jungle take these gods more seriously than they do Buddhism. They seem to attach more value to the power of the older gods to assist them in calamity; and they value oaths taken in their presence so highly that a man will often challenge his enemy to make oath in a *dewale*, and sometimes it is done at the command of a magistrate under the supervision of officers of the law courts. A man's oath may be welded to truth as he knows it in but two ways that I have seen either by honour or by superstition; and judging from the practice imposed in courts of justice in many lands, in houses of legislature and upon sovereigns at their accession, mankind in general does not hold honour to be the more binding method of the two. A Sinhalese villager who is challenged to swear before one of the older gods feels like an Englishman of the

Middle Ages did when exposed to trial by ordeal with High Heaven as umpire.

As in the water-holes, so in the older religion a great deal of Lanka's history lies hidden; and it must not be thought it is a trivial inquisitiveness, this peering into the superstitions of jungle villagers, for Ceylon, in that respect, may become the key to India, its mud and its godlings between them storing an epitome of the history of great movements of races. But the study will never be easy. These forest deities are immortal: they have lived through a hundred generations of men, but they are shy like forest animals, and it is as difficult to win their confidence. Some small study of the Veddhas has been made by peripatetic professors, and a friend of mine much given to exaggeration swears to having seen one learned investigator leave camp for a Veddha cave attired in (*a*) boots, (*b*) a green umbrella, and (*c*) a scarlet bathing costume. Not until some instructed man goes and lives among them will the jungle villagers who are not Veddhas yield their treasures of unconsciously stored knowledge; and for a man who is at the mercy of an interpreter it is a fruitless quest. I hope when it is done it will be by a Sinhalese trained in anthropology.

Among a people whose diet is partly hunted, and who have little to tender in exchange for imports, honey takes higher value than in

Europe at the present day. The body craves for sweets, as we found in Turkey during the later years of the war when sugar was almost impossibly costly for prisoners; and jungle men who grow very little sugar-cane rely on the forest for their sweets. Bee-rocks are important properties, and I expect some of these free sweet factories have been famous locally for many centuries, and that, like the water-holes, they might be worth probing for secrets; for bee-rocks, *bambara-gal* as they are called, are often associated with caves where human beings in the hunting stage could live luxuriously. None of the jungle folk of Ceylon are bee-keepers, but they help themselves systematically to wild honey, and are clever at finding hives. The large apis dorsata, the *bambara* bee, does not want much looking for. On some sheltered rock face, or beneath the bough of a tree in a nook protected from the wind, the swarm hangs without the smallest cover, and the comb is housed by the bodies of its citizens; and in some of these halting-places where they stay for about half of a year at a stretch, dozens of swarms live in close proximity, often almost touching.

I know one *bambara-gala* where a great rock that juts from the flank of a forest-covered hill overhangs its base and makes a refuge from the northerly winds, and here the bees hang in brown shimmering curtains that smell fiercely of the death that awaits their disturber, the scent of an infinite number of poisoned daggers. I crept up in the evening light with a man of the village that lies hidden in the forest hundreds of feet below, and we stood beneath the moving banners of the bees, and talked in low voices of their habits. With the aid of fire the jungle villagers deal as they please with the courageous insects, and always time their raids to come off before full moon, when, they say, the bees have a feast and drink their cellars dry, On the cliffs of Sigiriya, the famous rock fortress King Kasyapa lived in in the Sinhalese middle ages, a dozen swarms used to hang below inverted rock copings hundreds of feet above the level of the surrounding jungle, close by the rock ledges some found already perilous enough to climb. They often attacked people, and I have had to flee from them myself by paths it wanted a good head to follow in cold blood. Their most famous exploit was an onslaught on a royal party that visited Sigiriya more than twenty years ago, when a Royal Duchess was compelled to flee down steep stone steps into the jungle, and the Princess, her daughter, was actually marooned on the top of the rock until a bold man went up with the mosquito curtains off the rest-house beds and saved the situation. The funniest part of it, for the misadventures of others *are* funny, was when the Governor's daughter looked down the precipice and almost vertically below her saw her father, the representative of the king, pursuing his Majesty's sister-in-law and beating her with his hat. From that great height the bees were invisible, and for a moment or two the object of his tactics remained obscure.

The last time I climbed that rock the bees had gone, and a man of the village below told me they had been exterminated in a terrible war with the even more formidable hornets of the jungle. These strong brown and yellow insects build in the trees enormous nests of paper they manufacture from decayed wood, globular in form, and more than a yard in circumference. There were many such nests in the forest below the rock, and urged apparently by some common want described by the villager as concerted action, they rose in their millions and assaulted the swarms of *bambara* on the high cliff, and after several months of savage warfare waged high above earth, drove or killed them out, and spoiled their treasuries that had defied the efforts of men for one generation to my knowledge, and perhaps for scores, for they built a hundred feet above the tallest ladder, and were overhung by the out-leaning cliff above, but the hornets defeated them. The Sinhalese say that seven hornet stings equal in venom the bite of one cobra, but I have never heard of anyone being killed by them, though it is not very uncommon for people to be killed by *bambara* bees. When hornets build nests in the tea bushes Tamil coolies have a way of catching them which is quite easy but requires some nerve to attempt. Tea is a stiff little camelia bush kept neatly pruned, and the hornets begin to set up house in a small way with a nest about the size of a cricket ball in the midst of the hedge-like growth. It has only one entrance, and is easily crushed, but there is always, so far as I have seen, a sentinel hornet who patrols round and round the paper ball, and you have to wait until he is on the other side, at the antipodes, so to say, of your point of attack, before you go over the top. Then, with both hands in a doubled-up *kumbli,* the black Tamil blanket, you catch the ball and crush it in the folds. As a ball of that size will contain a tidy lot of hornets, and bearing in mind that you are potentially handling one-seventh part of that number of live cobras, you are naturally careful not to get tangled up in the branches. I should never have dared to do it if an almost naked Tamil had not shown me how. It is a difficult thing to assess courage, but one cannot withhold respect from a man who does what one fears to do oneself, especially if one is aware of feeling braver with clothes on.

Later in life, when my jungle days were

nearly over, I had an office in Kandy, and *bambara* bees lived in the verandah. At one time there were as many as nine swarms there and in the niches of the windows. They used to go away for about half the year, and they never did any harm despite some temptation; but sometimes they frightened people. Something disturbed them one day, and the whole nine swarms went off like a shell, and filled the garden and the adjoining street with the music of their dizzy circles until they settled, one swarm choosing a low branch close to the road and not far from my window. It was too tempting, and at last I could resist no longer, but went and looked at them close by. They seemed calm, and I put out my hand and touched them gently, and then, allured by the strange feel of it, put my whole hand into the swarm and held it there. The reward was notable, for I experienced a sensation entirely new to me, one of the half-dozen physical feelings that is entirely distinct from all others, and very pleasing. It was warm and rustling and dry, soft, and polished, and marvellously alive with the clinging of a myriad microscopic vacuum cleaners. I returned to my desk and wrote a few letters, but like a dram-drinker unable to resist temptation, once more went out, and this time bathed both hands in the vital cone of bees. An old Sinhalese man looked on from the road, and said, "Sir, they will sting you!" To which I replied, mindful of the prestige of my kind, "They never sting those who are free from all sin." But the old man was far from simple, for he wagged his beard and looked doubtful, and said, "Then they *will* sting you."

Sinhalese jungle men take the honey of a smaller bee than the *bambara*, and prefer its honey. As a rule these bees live in holes in trees and build up the entrance with propolis to leave one narrow way in, and to that small postern the jungle man places his mouth firmly and blows steadily. At first the bees hum loudly, but in a few minutes they seem to become subdued, and then he takes his axe and coolly cuts out the honey. Nothing is chewed first, and the spell is worked by the power of human breath alone. It is rather terrifying the first time one does it, for these bees can sting; but it is perfectly easy, and I have never known it to miscarry.

There is a still smaller bee who collects honey but who has no sting. She is not, however, quite without defence, for she can bite, and I have had a little collar of them biting my neck while I robbed their tiny hive; but the bites are not poisonous, and hurt less than gnats'. Jungle folk are connoisseurs of honey, and its use enters into their medical practice. Since beet-sugar is comparatively a modern luxury, and cane-sugar a product of the tropics,

I have sometimes wondered what housewives did in England before we traded with tropical regions. In 1918 the Turks fell back on honey, sold in wicker cylinders, and perhaps it was the universal sweetener in Europe a few hundred years ago.

I fancy that birds meddle with bees more than is always recognised, for I stood one day below a cliff watching the evolutions of an Indian Peregrine falcon, and wondering what he was thinking of, when suddenly he swooped at a *bambara* swarm and struck it with his talons. I could not see whether he succeeded in carrying off a bit of the brood comb, as was his aim I imagine, but in an instant the bees were streaming up after him in full cry as he swerved out and upward in the curve of his superb flight, and down again like a comet's tail as he slanted towards the jungle far below with gathering velocity. The end of that chase I could not follow, for when it swept over the spur where I stood the bees were diverted to me, and I had to flee for my life. Another time I stood on a steep hillside, and was puzzled by the movements of a small hawk who doubled and twisted in his flight as though pursued by harpies. Nothing was visible, and the bird seemed demented, until he swerved and passed close above my head, when I was able to see two fierce hornets following closely with equal flight, and conforming to every twist and double as they manœuvred for position to implant their stings. The hunt went too fast, and I did not see the finish.

But to go back to primitive man: I think the shelters among bee-haunted cliffs would yield remains of some sort, as would the floors of the caves where esculent swifts build their gummy nests, that are found right up in the highest hills near the *patanas*, the grass lands where so many deposits of crystal flakes have been observed. So common are the flakes that one has only to climb almost any of the steep breast-like hills, and poke about in the thin grass on the top to find them. The hill-top, especially if water runs in the valley below it, is nearly always littered with flakes of crystal that must have been carried there; for they are not natural to the site, and the few cores one finds show the flakes to be struck from water-worn pebbles rolled in old river valleys. The tops of these hills are rounded, and it is only on the top that the flakes are found, and as far down the sides as might be expected from random wash. I believe they are never found in the valleys, or even on the slopes, except quite near the top. On the *patanas* it is not difficult to find them, but in forest it is impossible because of the leaves and humus; nevertheless they are there all the same, and I have grown to believe that they exist more or less all over the hill country of Ceylon in such numbers as to prove that their makers were very numerous indeed. This does not mean, of course, that a hunting stone-age population was ever more than very thin, but that the same kind of people existed over a very long period of time, and that they changed their ground often. Proof that flakes exist in the forest is to be found in the tea and rubber estates, many of which were forest less than a hundred years ago: then they were cleared, roads and drains were cut, holes were dug, and coffee was planted. And when coffee died out in the eighteen eighties tea was planted, and this meant reholing the land and other earth-shifting operations. Later on rubber came on the scene, sometimes planted on new forest lands, sometimes on old tea lands, and sometimes on *chenas* where shifting cultivation had been practised for centuries; and it all meant lifting soil and exposing crystal flakes. I have hunted for them in a dozen different districts, and hardly ever failed to find at least a few; and always in similar situations, on the tops of hills or hillocks not very far from water. Dr Hrdlicka, editor of the American journal of 'Anthropology,' with whom I had the fortune to discuss these flakes, describes them as approaching later palæolithic forms. To me the fascination has ever lain in the effort to cast back on the trail of those bygone men, to endeavour to regain some particle of their outlook on life, some little scene from the dreams they dreamed on their hill-tops by the singing mountain streams. Did they dwell on hill-tops for safety, with stockades around their summits; or was it simply that the valleys were damp and full of frogs who attracted serpents who bit the palæolithic children. If anyone reads this who would care to carry his interest further, he may start almost anywhere in Dikoya or Maskeliya or South Matale and find flakes on the nearest suitable spot; or he may leave the train at Peradeniya station and follow the river up-stream towards Gampola, finding deposits on every hillock by the way; or from the hotel at Bandarawela he may stroll into the folds of the downs and find as many there as anywhere else in Ceylon.

Perhaps the surest way to recapture the outlook of palæolithic man is to do as he did, and to hunt the game he hunted without accepting the aid of modern weapons. When the elk-hounds meet, and planters hunt sambhur on foot through the jungles of the Norton Plains seven thousand feet above sea-level, running over the *patanas*, struggling through thick *nilu* undergrowth, and finishing the bay in a deep cold pool of the mountain stream with a knife thrust through the heart, they are not far in spirit from the men whose crystal flakes strew the hills around them.

In remote jungles of the eastern province brown men still run bravely afoot and noose wild buffaloes and even wild elephants by hand, and tame them afterwards; and in a more humble way I, too, once hunted with no weapons but those available even to eolithic man. It happened thus. Two young Moormen and I took a bee-line through jungle-covered hills, and when we came to a fine stream halted and bathed, they in the strips of calico Eastern men wear, and I in shorts. There were shoals of small fish there, so tame that we caught them in our hands and let them go again; after which they returned and nibbled my body, and I found that what they were after was minute provender of some kind that drifted down-stream and lodged against my white skin where it could be the more easily seen and captured; but it felt as if they had decided to eat me alive as the rats ate Bishop Hatto, not painful, but a unique kind of tickle. It was in that glade of Arcady that the hunt developed, and our quarry was almost a dragon. There were many rocks in the stream bed, with deep pools between them, and little rapids and waterfalls between the pools; and as we went exploring we put up a *kabaragoya*, a huge amphibious lizard four or five feet in length, who fled into the nearest covert where the stream ran rapidly through a narrow filled with boulders. *Kabaragoyas* are the creatures whose skins are made into ladies' shoes. They are flesh-eating animals, very strong, fairly swift, and armed with sharp teeth and a whiplash tail. We hunted him just as we were, swimming, wading, plunging deep among the rocks, and following him as hotly as hounds follow an otter. He never attempted to leave the stream, but he led us a chase from pool to rapid and rapid to waterfall, until at last I tailed him as he dived between two boulders. It took the three of us to drag him out, and before his head could whip round and seize one of us we slew him like Goliath with a smooth stone from the bottom of the stream; and that was the most utterly primitive hunt I ever took part in. Except that we were three to one it was fair fighting, as rifles can never be; but we did not eat him, and perhaps it was a cruel thing to kill him merely to fulfil a throw-back instinct. If men could bring their ethics of killing up to the level of the hunting animals and only slay for food, the jungle might retain its wonderful balance of life for centuries to come: but in the long-run it looks as though the best hope for the more beautiful animals may lie in human population becoming stationary before we require the whole surface of the earth for growing food for factory hands.

The *patanas* I have briefly mentioned have always been looked upon as natural features of the hill country. Right up to their edges the forest grows unstinted, and then, without any gradual ending off in bushes or small trees, its place is taken by grass where harebells grow, and pink and yellow orchids. In the high hills, above five thousand feet elevation, the *patanas* are dotted with rhododendron trees in ones and tens and groves, not close generally, but spaced like the trees in an abandoned orchard; and the sight of a group of these, radiant with crimson blossom, makes one stop and take a deep breath in the half-conscious effort to absorb the whole joy of such unrivalled beauty. Lower down another tree, the *kahata*, takes the rhododendron's place in the *patanas*.

I am doubtful whether the *patanas* are natural. It seems to me more probable that they were the clearings of the men who chipped the crystals. It used to be supposed that forest would not grow on *patana* land, and tea-planters avoided it; but now tea has been successfully grown on many a *patana*, its neat rows taking the place of the scattered rhododendrons, and the foresters have made plantations of fast-growing Australian trees for fire-wood, wattles, and the like, on *patana* lands previously scorned. It is the fire-resisting power of seedling rhododendrons and *kahatas* that enables them to live out in the open. The evergreen forests of Ceylon will not burn as do the resinous woods of colder climes; and I have seen a fire rage through long ripe grass in the height of the dry weather in the low country, only to halt at the edge of light forest, unable to do more than lick up a few of the nearest fallen leaves. *Patanas* are frequently set afire, for the grass which springs anew is soft and rich for the cattle who roam half-wild; and in the plains, park lands are burned for the same reason, and also to ease the search for shed antlers. Thus none but fire-resisting trees can start life amid the grass, though they can maintain their position fairly well if once grown to even half their height; so reafforestation is indefinitely postponed, and the fact that it is a very long time since palæolithic man flaked crystals is no reason why his clearings should not remain as grass, provided he used fire. The parallel of the *patanas* in the plains lies in the so-called park lands, and in many cases it is evident that parks were but the fields below tanks abandoned soon after the twelfth century A.D. They are not quite so slow to reafforest themselves, for trees soon grow along the banks of old channels, and in hollows where water lodges in wet weather as it cannot lodge on the steep sides of the *patanas;* but, even so, five hundred years will not serve to make a field into high forest.

The periodical burnings must affect the fauna in the same direction as the flora; only the fire-resisting creatures can survive; swift things like the larger animals, things strong of wing, and things that can burrow deep. Snakes, for the most part, are destroyed annually, and only reinvade such lands from surrounding territory after the day of judgment. The distribution of snakes is, of course, governed largely by their food supply, and we used to find a great many among the ruins, for nooks and corners and ancient ponds made homes for the birds and bats and lizards and frogs they preyed on. I remember one day walking among ruins with a stoutly-built gentleman who had invented Oxford trousers a score of years before Oxford did, and all went well until something ran up his leg. He stopped dead, and we debated how to dislodge this creature—snake, scorpion, or centipede, or perhaps a tarantula—without inciting it to bite or sting. For all we knew it might be deadly. There were two living beings in a garment only meant for one, and the question was who should be got out first. Finally we decided to evacuate the human garrison. I managed to isolate the invader in an outlying bulge of the flannel round which I slipped a noose and pulled it tight; then the human being stepped delicately out of the danger zone, and we turned it inside out, and released the unknown from his prison. He turned out to be a harmless lizard.

If the *patanas* are the old clearings of the men of the crystal flakes, and the park lands the fields of the last great Buddhist kings, there are lands lost by the British which already do not greatly differ from them in character. Coffee was king until a time within the memory of men still planting, but a scale insect and a fungoid disease attacked it simultaneously and wiped it out. There is now no coffee in Ceylon, and tens of thousands of acres where once it grew are now grassy wilderness fast settling down into the abandoned state of the park and *patana* lands. I know a valley where no Briton lives now, where the villagers show a wind-blown down as the old race-course of the coffee planters of half a century ago. A rock-girt hill beside it, hard for men to climb, is the abode of a god of the older religion, one Gange Bandara, in whose honour invisible drums are beaten by inhuman hands each Friday night. One cannot but wonder if he, too, was once as real and full of blood as the planters of the race-course who are already becoming legendary. The night I slept in the valley below these two strangely different haunts of fading story I heard the *Ullama* cry loudly, a dreadful shriek, and the mother of many terrors. Its ghost seems at long last to have been laid by an adventurous Ceylonese doctor who tracked it down and shot it, only to find that the demon had changed into a hawk-eagle. But in the village, people answered its cry, echoing its horror in the hope that thus by hollow pretence the devil-bird might be satisfied, and depart without claiming a life. A child was born the night I heard it, and the poor mother listened anxiously as the sounds passed by her little hut.

In this village, once close neighbour to a flourishing district where coffee planters made and spent fortunes, the jungle tide has flowed. Lantana scrub covers the old coffee fields, and wild pigs grub where women used to weed. But taking Ceylon as a whole, it is not easy to say whether the tide has ebbed or flowed the more since history began there. Coffee has gone, and much ground it grew on has lain idle for forty years; but tea and rubber fill a larger area than ever coffee did. The old kingdom of the plains is a forest now, but the fields round Colombo were forests then; at least I think they were, though the discovery of Roman coins of the later empire when the battery on Galle Face was built makes it less than certain. Tea has covered many of the higher hills, but the crystal flake men were there long before tea was ever exported from China. Even now I do not feel certain that civilisation will win, though to believe so is a truism of modern thought.

One cannot steal the secrets of nature, nor beg or borrow them either. As a rule they must be worked for very hard, as hard as Manson and Ross worked before the secret of malaria was unravelled, and the strongest dragon who protected the wondrous life of tropical forests defanged. Maeterlinck, in his 'Life of the White Ant,' says that those insects have "rendered certain parts of . . . Ceylon uncultivable; the struggle there has been given up." For nearly thirty years I walked most parts of Ceylon, and I believe he is entirely wrong as a historian: no part of Ceylon has been abandoned on account of white ants; but he may be right as a prophet. Calotermes, a white ant that can assimilate living plant tissue as well as dead, has taken to tea as eagerly as planters hoped the Americans would when they outlawed alcohol the destroyer. Calotermes may form an alliance with a fungus, and the combine might prove fatal, as with coffee. It is only a remote possibility at present. It is unlikely that man will be unable to kill calotermes when he wants to, and the point is less that than how much will it cost? If it costs more to save a bush than the capital value of the bush when saved, then the conflict may not be prosecuted, and some areas of tea may follow coffee under the jungle tide. With malaria, too, it is the cost that counts. The Panama Canal was so stupendous a project that the cost of freeing that priceless strip of land from mosquitoes was a mere bagatelle, but it is no guide to operations elsewhere. Where it costs more to rid land of malaria than the land is worth when ridded, the operation will be postponed until mankind wants the land so badly that it cannot do without it, until, in fact, the land is worth more than it costs. In India, where civilisation is so old, the rule of the British has coincided with an increase in the population of about one hundred million souls, and a relative rolling back of the jungle tide. It is usually tacitly assumed that this process will continue indefinitely until the whole world has been tamed by man. Natural selection is to be superseded by man's selection, and evolution suspended where it does not serve his purpose. Gardens are to take the place of jungles, tame beasts to live in place of wild, and revolt to be supplanted by obedience. Plants will but pollinate and beasts mate by special licence as on a stud farm, and weeds will be as rare as at a flower show. This is the theme of several very thoughtful books; but I think of the crystal flake men, of the buried cities of the Buddhist kings, and of the wealthy coffee industry, and I feel doubtful; hopefully doubtful, for a world without revolt would be one to fly from, even in one of those vaunted rocket-driven planes that are to reach the moon, there to trust to whatever gods may breathe its thin airs to supply new rockets to come back with, or to fly on farther.

British imperialism is dying. Its motive force was individual excellence, heroism if you like, and we are pledged to its opposite, to the wisdom of the average man which may be an amiable thing but cannot possibly be the same as the wisdom of men who are *not* average. It looks as though we were going to leave the Nessus shirt of government by discussion behind us as our parting gift to the Asiatics we have ruled so long and so efficiently; and then to stand aside and watch them take the front rank in the eternal struggle with the jungle. For the jungle tide always strives to flow, and ebbs no more than it is actually pushed back; and the fight cannot end until plants cease to seed. Our rule has been so efficient that it has caused the indigenous efficiency of southern Asia to atrophy. Our hothouse methods have forced growth in protected populations and left them soft through lack of the real struggle of life, and now we turn off the hot water and invite them to grow in the open. The next century will see the result, and it will be a mighty interesting experiment; but it seems a dangerous thing to subject to experiment the very existence of a population as numerous as that of North America, which is about what we have added to Asia; and it is an experiment politicians can enter upon more light-heartedly than would biologists. The better the government by aliens, the more paralysing its check to the natural advance of the governed, and a thoughtful Indian might rather risk being himself among the hundred millions jeopardised, than leave it to his grandson to be one of an unwanted two hundred millions. There are some situations the wisdom of man cannot mend, and he must fall back on the primitive virtues of courage and fortitude to win through them.

Visions of a regimented earth where birds only sing by request are to me so much more distasteful than the age-old struggle with the jungle tide, that I rejoice in an outlook that seems to the commercial utiliser of applied science horribly pessimistic. I do not think man will win final victory over the jungle; but rather that the battle will go on in the future as it has in the past with alternating victories on either side, and with the tide of the jungle ever ready to rise and flow over civilisation whenever it grows too proud to keep on learning, as Spain once grew; or when it gets tired of exerting will-power, as we seem to be doing; or when it makes mistakes, as the Sinhalese kings did when they pinned their prosperity to a vulnerable irrigation system.

CREDO

MOUNTAINS, and woods, and the winds that blow over them;
Meadows, and downs, and the wild flowers that cover them;
Rocks, and ravines, and the jungles that smother them;
    All these I love with a love that possesseth me,
    But more than all of these I worship thee.

Sea, and the shore, and shells the gods squander there;
Corals, and pools, and wild things that wander there;
Silence, and caves, and the thoughts that men ponder there;
    All these I love with a love that enchanteth me,
    But deeper in my depths springs love for thee.